C-3473   CAREER EXAMINATION SERIES

This is your
PASSBOOK for...

Senior Clerical Series

Test Preparation Study Guide
Questions & Answers

COPYRIGHT NOTICE

This book is SOLELY intended for, is sold ONLY to, and its use is RESTRICTED to individual, bona fide applicants or candidates who qualify by virtue of having seriously filed applications for appropriate license, certificate, professional and/or promotional advancement, higher school matriculation, scholarship, or other legitimate requirements of education and/or governmental authorities.

This book is NOT intended for use, class instruction, tutoring, training, duplication, copying, reprinting, excerption, or adaptation, etc., by:

1) Other publishers
2) Proprietors and/or Instructors of "Coaching" and/or Preparatory Courses
3) Personnel and/or Training Divisions of commercial, industrial, and governmental organizations
4) Schools, colleges, or universities and/or their departments and staffs, including teachers and other personnel
5) Testing Agencies or Bureaus
6) Study groups which seek by the purchase of a single volume to copy and/or duplicate and/or adapt this material for use by the group as a whole without having purchased individual volumes for each of the members of the group
7) Et al.

Such persons would be in violation of appropriate Federal and State statutes.

PROVISION OF LICENSING AGREEMENTS – Recognized educational, commercial, industrial, and governmental institutions and organizations, and others legitimately engaged in educational pursuits, including training, testing, and measurement activities, may address request for a licensing agreement to the copyright owners, who will determine whether, and under what conditions, including fees and charges, the materials in this book may be used them. In other words, a licensing facility exists for the legitimate use of the material in this book on other than an individual basis. However, it is asseverated and affirmed here that the material in this book CANNOT be used without the receipt of the express permission of such a licensing agreement from the Publishers. Inquiries re licensing should be addressed to the company, attention rights and permissions department.

All rights reserved, including the right of reproduction in whole or in part, in any form or by any means, electronic or mechanical, including photocopying, recording, or by any information storage and retrieval system, without permission in writing from the Publisher.

Copyright © 2024 by
National Learning Corporation

212 Michael Drive, Syosset, NY 11791
(516) 921-8888 • www.passbooks.com
E-mail: info@passbooks.com

PUBLISHED IN THE UNITED STATES OF AMERICA

PASSBOOK® SERIES

THE *PASSBOOK® SERIES* has been created to prepare applicants and candidates for the ultimate academic battlefield – the examination room.

At some time in our lives, each and every one of us may be required to take an examination – for validation, matriculation, admission, qualification, registration, certification, or licensure.

Based on the assumption that every applicant or candidate has met the basic formal educational standards, has taken the required number of courses, and read the necessary texts, the *PASSBOOK® SERIES* furnishes the one special preparation which may assure passing with confidence, instead of failing with insecurity. Examination questions – together with answers – are furnished as the basic vehicle for study so that the mysteries of the examination and its compounding difficulties may be eliminated or diminished by a sure method.

This book is meant to help you pass your examination provided that you qualify and are serious in your objective.

The entire field is reviewed through the huge store of content information which is succinctly presented through a provocative and challenging approach – the question-and-answer method.

A climate of success is established by furnishing the correct answers at the end of each test.

You soon learn to recognize types of questions, forms of questions, and patterns of questioning. You may even begin to anticipate expected outcomes.

You perceive that many questions are repeated or adapted so that you can gain acute insights, which may enable you to score many sure points.

You learn how to confront new questions, or types of questions, and to attack them confidently and work out the correct answers.

You note objectives and emphases, and recognize pitfalls and dangers, so that you may make positive educational adjustments.

Moreover, you are kept fully informed in relation to new concepts, methods, practices, and directions in the field.

You discover that you are actually taking the examination all the time: you are preparing for the examination by "taking" an examination, not by reading extraneous and/or supererogatory textbooks.

In short, this PASSBOOK®, used directedly, should be an important factor in helping you to pass your test.

SENIOR CLERICAL SERIES

DUTIES
This examination fills various senior level clerical positions including clerks, typists, stenographers, and office workers. Incumbents in these positions may supervise and/or perform all clerical activities in a department such as composing all typing, correspondence, vouchers, reports, or other materials. Also, may act as secretary to agency or department head.

SUBJECT OF EXAMINATION
The written test will be designed to test for knowledge, skills, and/or abilities in such areas as:
1. Office practices;
2. Office record keeping;
3. Keyboarding practices;
4. English grammar, usage and punctuation; and
5. Spelling.

HOW TO TAKE A TEST

I. YOU MUST PASS AN EXAMINATION

A. *WHAT EVERY CANDIDATE SHOULD KNOW*

Examination applicants often ask us for help in preparing for the written test. What can I study in advance? What kinds of questions will be asked? How will the test be given? How will the papers be graded?

As an applicant for a civil service examination, you may be wondering about some of these things. Our purpose here is to suggest effective methods of advance study and to describe civil service examinations.

Your chances for success on this examination can be increased if you know how to prepare. Those "pre-examination jitters" can be reduced if you know what to expect. You can even experience an adventure in good citizenship if you know why civil service exams are given.

B. *WHY ARE CIVIL SERVICE EXAMINATIONS GIVEN?*

Civil service examinations are important to you in two ways. As a citizen, you want public jobs filled by employees who know how to do their work. As a job seeker, you want a fair chance to compete for that job on an equal footing with other candidates. The best-known means of accomplishing this two-fold goal is the competitive examination.

Exams are widely publicized throughout the nation. They may be administered for jobs in federal, state, city, municipal, town or village governments or agencies.

Any citizen may apply, with some limitations, such as the age or residence of applicants. Your experience and education may be reviewed to see whether you meet the requirements for the particular examination. When these requirements exist, they are reasonable and applied consistently to all applicants. Thus, a competitive examination may cause you some uneasiness now, but it is your privilege and safeguard.

C. *HOW ARE CIVIL SERVICE EXAMS DEVELOPED?*

Examinations are carefully written by trained technicians who are specialists in the field known as "psychological measurement," in consultation with recognized authorities in the field of work that the test will cover. These experts recommend the subject matter areas or skills to be tested; only those knowledges or skills important to your success on the job are included. The most reliable books and source materials available are used as references. Together, the experts and technicians judge the difficulty level of the questions.

Test technicians know how to phrase questions so that the problem is clearly stated. Their ethics do not permit "trick" or "catch" questions. Questions may have been tried out on sample groups, or subjected to statistical analysis, to determine their usefulness.

Written tests are often used in combination with performance tests, ratings of training and experience, and oral interviews. All of these measures combine to form the best-known means of finding the right person for the right job.

II. HOW TO PASS THE WRITTEN TEST

A. NATURE OF THE EXAMINATION

To prepare intelligently for civil service examinations, you should know how they differ from school examinations you have taken. In school you were assigned certain definite pages to read or subjects to cover. The examination questions were quite detailed and usually emphasized memory. Civil service exams, on the other hand, try to discover your present ability to perform the duties of a position, plus your potentiality to learn these duties. In other words, a civil service exam attempts to predict how successful you will be. Questions cover such a broad area that they cannot be as minute and detailed as school exam questions.

In the public service similar kinds of work, or positions, are grouped together in one "class." This process is known as *position-classification*. All the positions in a class are paid according to the salary range for that class. One class title covers all of these positions, and they are all tested by the same examination.

B. FOUR BASIC STEPS

1) Study the announcement

How, then, can you know what subjects to study? Our best answer is: "Learn as much as possible about the class of positions for which you've applied." The exam will test the knowledge, skills and abilities needed to do the work.

Your most valuable source of information about the position you want is the official exam announcement. This announcement lists the training and experience qualifications. Check these standards and apply only if you come reasonably close to meeting them.

The brief description of the position in the examination announcement offers some clues to the subjects which will be tested. Think about the job itself. Review the duties in your mind. Can you perform them, or are there some in which you are rusty? Fill in the blank spots in your preparation.

Many jurisdictions preview the written test in the exam announcement by including a section called "Knowledge and Abilities Required," "Scope of the Examination," or some similar heading. Here you will find out specifically what fields will be tested.

2) Review your own background

Once you learn in general what the position is all about, and what you need to know to do the work, ask yourself which subjects you already know fairly well and which need improvement. You may wonder whether to concentrate on improving your strong areas or on building some background in your fields of weakness. When the announcement has specified "some knowledge" or "considerable knowledge," or has used adjectives like "beginning principles of…" or "advanced … methods," you can get a clue as to the number and difficulty of questions to be asked in any given field. More questions, and hence broader coverage, would be included for those subjects which are more important in the work. Now weigh your strengths and weaknesses against the job requirements and prepare accordingly.

3) Determine the level of the position

Another way to tell how intensively you should prepare is to understand the level of the job for which you are applying. Is it the entering level? In other words, is this the position in which beginners in a field of work are hired? Or is it an intermediate or advanced level? Sometimes this is indicated by such words as "Junior" or "Senior" in the class title. Other jurisdictions use Roman numerals to designate the level – Clerk I, Clerk II, for example. The word "Supervisor" sometimes appears in the title. If the level is not indicated by the title, check the description of duties. Will you be working under very close supervision, or will you have responsibility for independent decisions in this work?

4) Choose appropriate study materials

Now that you know the subjects to be examined and the relative amount of each subject to be covered, you can choose suitable study materials. For beginning level jobs, or even advanced ones, if you have a pronounced weakness in some aspect of your training, read a modern, standard textbook in that field. Be sure it is up to date and has general coverage. Such books are normally available at your library, and the librarian will be glad to help you locate one. For entry-level positions, questions of appropriate difficulty are chosen – neither highly advanced questions, nor those too simple. Such questions require careful thought but not advanced training.

If the position for which you are applying is technical or advanced, you will read more advanced, specialized material. If you are already familiar with the basic principles of your field, elementary textbooks would waste your time. Concentrate on advanced textbooks and technical periodicals. Think through the concepts and review difficult problems in your field.

These are all general sources. You can get more ideas on your own initiative, following these leads. For example, training manuals and publications of the government agency which employs workers in your field can be useful, particularly for technical and professional positions. A letter or visit to the government department involved may result in more specific study suggestions, and certainly will provide you with a more definite idea of the exact nature of the position you are seeking.

III. KINDS OF TESTS

Tests are used for purposes other than measuring knowledge and ability to perform specified duties. For some positions, it is equally important to test ability to make adjustments to new situations or to profit from training. In others, basic mental abilities not dependent on information are essential. Questions which test these things may not appear as pertinent to the duties of the position as those which test for knowledge and information. Yet they are often highly important parts of a fair examination. For very general questions, it is almost impossible to help you direct your study efforts. What we can do is to point out some of the more common of these general abilities needed in public service positions and describe some typical questions.

1) General information

Broad, general information has been found useful for predicting job success in some kinds of work. This is tested in a variety of ways, from vocabulary lists to questions about current events. Basic background in some field of work, such as sociology or economics, may be sampled in a group of questions. Often these are principles which have become familiar to most persons through exposure rather than through formal training. It is difficult to advise you how to study for these questions; being alert to the world around you is our best suggestion.

2) Verbal ability

An example of an ability needed in many positions is verbal or language ability. Verbal ability is, in brief, the ability to use and understand words. Vocabulary and grammar tests are typical measures of this ability. Reading comprehension or paragraph interpretation questions are common in many kinds of civil service tests. You are given a paragraph of written material and asked to find its central meaning.

3) Numerical ability

Number skills can be tested by the familiar arithmetic problem, by checking paired lists of numbers to see which are alike and which are different, or by interpreting charts and graphs. In the latter test, a graph may be printed in the test booklet which you are asked to use as the basis for answering questions.

4) Observation

A popular test for law-enforcement positions is the observation test. A picture is shown to you for several minutes, then taken away. Questions about the picture test your ability to observe both details and larger elements.

5) Following directions

In many positions in the public service, the employee must be able to carry out written instructions dependably and accurately. You may be given a chart with several columns, each column listing a variety of information. The questions require you to carry out directions involving the information given in the chart.

6) Skills and aptitudes

Performance tests effectively measure some manual skills and aptitudes. When the skill is one in which you are trained, such as typing or shorthand, you can practice. These tests are often very much like those given in business school or high school courses. For many of the other skills and aptitudes, however, no short-time preparation can be made. Skills and abilities natural to you or that you have developed throughout your lifetime are being tested.

Many of the general questions just described provide all the data needed to answer the questions and ask you to use your reasoning ability to find the answers. Your best preparation for these tests, as well as for tests of facts and ideas, is to be at your physical and mental best. You, no doubt, have your own methods of getting into an exam-taking mood and keeping "in shape." The next section lists some ideas on this subject.

IV. KINDS OF QUESTIONS

Only rarely is the "essay" question, which you answer in narrative form, used in civil service tests. Civil service tests are usually of the short-answer type. Full instructions for answering these questions will be given to you at the examination. But in case this is your first experience with short-answer questions and separate answer sheets, here is what you need to know:

1) **Multiple-choice Questions**

Most popular of the short-answer questions is the "multiple choice" or "best answer" question. It can be used, for example, to test for factual knowledge, ability to solve problems or judgment in meeting situations found at work.

A multiple-choice question is normally one of three types—
- It can begin with an incomplete statement followed by several possible endings. You are to find the one ending which *best* completes the statement, although some of the others may not be entirely wrong.
- It can also be a complete statement in the form of a question which is answered by choosing one of the statements listed.

- It can be in the form of a problem – again you select the best answer.

Here is an example of a multiple-choice question with a discussion which should give you some clues as to the method for choosing the right answer:

When an employee has a complaint about his assignment, the action which will *best* help him overcome his difficulty is to
- A. discuss his difficulty with his coworkers
- B. take the problem to the head of the organization
- C. take the problem to the person who gave him the assignment
- D. say nothing to anyone about his complaint

In answering this question, you should study each of the choices to find which is best. Consider choice "A" – Certainly an employee may discuss his complaint with fellow employees, but no change or improvement can result, and the complaint remains unresolved. Choice "B" is a poor choice since the head of the organization probably does not know what assignment you have been given, and taking your problem to him is known as "going over the head" of the supervisor. The supervisor, or person who made the assignment, is the person who can clarify it or correct any injustice. Choice "C" is, therefore, correct. To say nothing, as in choice "D," is unwise. Supervisors have and interest in knowing the problems employees are facing, and the employee is seeking a solution to his problem.

2) True/False Questions

The "true/false" or "right/wrong" form of question is sometimes used. Here a complete statement is given. Your job is to decide whether the statement is right or wrong.

SAMPLE: A roaming cell-phone call to a nearby city costs less than a non-roaming call to a distant city.

This statement is wrong, or false, since roaming calls are more expensive.

This is not a complete list of all possible question forms, although most of the others are variations of these common types. You will always get complete directions for answering questions. Be sure you understand *how* to mark your answers – ask questions until you do.

V. RECORDING YOUR ANSWERS

Computer terminals are used more and more today for many different kinds of exams.

For an examination with very few applicants, you may be told to record your answers in the test booklet itself. Separate answer sheets are much more common. If this separate answer sheet is to be scored by machine – and this is often the case – it is highly important that you mark your answers correctly in order to get credit.

An electronic scoring machine is often used in civil service offices because of the speed with which papers can be scored. Machine-scored answer sheets must be marked with a pencil, which will be given to you. This pencil has a high graphite content which responds to the electronic scoring machine. As a matter of fact, stray dots may register as answers, so do not let your pencil rest on the answer sheet while you are pondering the correct answer. Also, if your pencil lead breaks or is otherwise defective, ask for another.

Since the answer sheet will be dropped in a slot in the scoring machine, be careful not to bend the corners or get the paper crumpled.

The answer sheet normally has five vertical columns of numbers, with 30 numbers to a column. These numbers correspond to the question numbers in your test booklet. After each number, going across the page are four or five pairs of dotted lines. These short dotted lines have small letters or numbers above them. The first two pairs may also have a "T" or "F" above the letters. This indicates that the first two pairs only are to be used if the questions are of the true-false type. If the questions are multiple choice, disregard the "T" and "F" and pay attention only to the small letters or numbers.

Answer your questions in the manner of the sample that follows:

32. The largest city in the United States is
 A. Washington, D.C.
 B. New York City
 C. Chicago
 D. Detroit
 E. San Francisco

1) Choose the answer you think is best. (New York City is the largest, so "B" is correct.)
2) Find the row of dotted lines numbered the same as the question you are answering. (Find row number 32)
3) Find the pair of dotted lines corresponding to the answer. (Find the pair of lines under the mark "B.")
4) Make a solid black mark between the dotted lines.

VI. BEFORE THE TEST

Common sense will help you find procedures to follow to get ready for an examination. Too many of us, however, overlook these sensible measures. Indeed, nervousness and fatigue have been found to be the most serious reasons why applicants fail to do their best on civil service tests. Here is a list of reminders:

- Begin your preparation early – Don't wait until the last minute to go scurrying around for books and materials or to find out what the position is all about.
- Prepare continuously – An hour a night for a week is better than an all-night cram session. This has been definitely established. What is more, a night a week for a month will return better dividends than crowding your study into a shorter period of time.
- Locate the place of the exam – You have been sent a notice telling you when and where to report for the examination. If the location is in a different town or otherwise unfamiliar to you, it would be well to inquire the best route and learn something about the building.
- Relax the night before the test – Allow your mind to rest. Do not study at all that night. Plan some mild recreation or diversion; then go to bed early and get a good night's sleep.
- Get up early enough to make a leisurely trip to the place for the test – This way unforeseen events, traffic snarls, unfamiliar buildings, etc. will not upset you.
- Dress comfortably – A written test is not a fashion show. You will be known by number and not by name, so wear something comfortable.

- Leave excess paraphernalia at home – Shopping bags and odd bundles will get in your way. You need bring only the items mentioned in the official notice you received; usually everything you need is provided. Do not bring reference books to the exam. They will only confuse those last minutes and be taken away from you when in the test room.
- Arrive somewhat ahead of time – If because of transportation schedules you must get there very early, bring a newspaper or magazine to take your mind off yourself while waiting.
- Locate the examination room – When you have found the proper room, you will be directed to the seat or part of the room where you will sit. Sometimes you are given a sheet of instructions to read while you are waiting. Do not fill out any forms until you are told to do so; just read them and be prepared.
- Relax and prepare to listen to the instructions
- If you have any physical problem that may keep you from doing your best, be sure to tell the test administrator. If you are sick or in poor health, you really cannot do your best on the exam. You can come back and take the test some other time.

VII. AT THE TEST

The day of the test is here and you have the test booklet in your hand. The temptation to get going is very strong. Caution! There is more to success than knowing the right answers. You must know how to identify your papers and understand variations in the type of short-answer question used in this particular examination. Follow these suggestions for maximum results from your efforts:

1) Cooperate with the monitor
The test administrator has a duty to create a situation in which you can be as much at ease as possible. He will give instructions, tell you when to begin, check to see that you are marking your answer sheet correctly, and so on. He is not there to guard you, although he will see that your competitors do not take unfair advantage. He wants to help you do your best.

2) Listen to all instructions
Don't jump the gun! Wait until you understand all directions. In most civil service tests you get more time than you need to answer the questions. So don't be in a hurry. Read each word of instructions until you clearly understand the meaning. Study the examples, listen to all announcements and follow directions. Ask questions if you do not understand what to do.

3) Identify your papers
Civil service exams are usually identified by number only. You will be assigned a number; you must not put your name on your test papers. Be sure to copy your number correctly. Since more than one exam may be given, copy your exact examination title.

4) Plan your time
Unless you are told that a test is a "speed" or "rate of work" test, speed itself is usually not important. Time enough to answer all the questions will be provided, but this does not mean that you have all day. An overall time limit has been set. Divide the total time (in minutes) by the number of questions to determine the approximate time you have for each question.

5) Do not linger over difficult questions

If you come across a difficult question, mark it with a paper clip (useful to have along) and come back to it when you have been through the booklet. One caution if you do this – be sure to skip a number on your answer sheet as well. Check often to be sure that you have not lost your place and that you are marking in the row numbered the same as the question you are answering.

6) Read the questions

Be sure you know what the question asks! Many capable people are unsuccessful because they failed to *read* the questions correctly.

7) Answer all questions

Unless you have been instructed that a penalty will be deducted for incorrect answers, it is better to guess than to omit a question.

8) Speed tests

It is often better NOT to guess on speed tests. It has been found that on timed tests people are tempted to spend the last few seconds before time is called in marking answers at random – without even reading them – in the hope of picking up a few extra points. To discourage this practice, the instructions may warn you that your score will be "corrected" for guessing. That is, a penalty will be applied. The incorrect answers will be deducted from the correct ones, or some other penalty formula will be used.

9) Review your answers

If you finish before time is called, go back to the questions you guessed or omitted to give them further thought. Review other answers if you have time.

10) Return your test materials

If you are ready to leave before others have finished or time is called, take ALL your materials to the monitor and leave quietly. Never take any test material with you. The monitor can discover whose papers are not complete, and taking a test booklet may be grounds for disqualification.

VIII. EXAMINATION TECHNIQUES

1) Read the general instructions carefully. These are usually printed on the first page of the exam booklet. As a rule, these instructions refer to the timing of the examination; the fact that you should not start work until the signal and must stop work at a signal, etc. If there are any *special* instructions, such as a choice of questions to be answered, make sure that you note this instruction carefully.

2) When you are ready to start work on the examination, that is as soon as the signal has been given, read the instructions to each question booklet, underline any key words or phrases, such as *least, best, outline, describe* and the like. In this way you will tend to answer as requested rather than discover on reviewing your paper that you *listed without describing*, that you selected the *worst* choice rather than the *best* choice, etc.

3) If the examination is of the objective or multiple-choice type – that is, each question will also give a series of possible answers: A, B, C or D, and you are called upon to select the best answer and write the letter next to that answer on your answer paper – it is advisable to start answering each question in turn. There may be anywhere from 50 to 100 such questions in the three or four hours allotted and you can see how much time would be taken if you read through all the questions before beginning to answer any. Furthermore, if you come across a question or group of questions which you know would be difficult to answer, it would undoubtedly affect your handling of all the other questions.

4) If the examination is of the essay type and contains but a few questions, it is a moot point as to whether you should read all the questions before starting to answer any one. Of course, if you are given a choice – say five out of seven and the like – then it is essential to read all the questions so you can eliminate the two that are most difficult. If, however, you are asked to answer all the questions, there may be danger in trying to answer the easiest one first because you may find that you will spend too much time on it. The best technique is to answer the first question, then proceed to the second, etc.

5) Time your answers. Before the exam begins, write down the time it started, then add the time allowed for the examination and write down the time it must be completed, then divide the time available somewhat as follows:
    - If 3-1/2 hours are allowed, that would be 210 minutes. If you have 80 objective-type questions, that would be an average of 2-1/2 minutes per question. Allow yourself no more than 2 minutes per question, or a total of 160 minutes, which will permit about 50 minutes to review.
    - If for the time allotment of 210 minutes there are 7 essay questions to answer, that would average about 30 minutes a question. Give yourself only 25 minutes per question so that you have about 35 minutes to review.

6) The most important instruction is to *read each question* and make sure you know what is wanted. The second most important instruction is to *time yourself properly* so that you answer every question. The third most important instruction is to *answer every question*. Guess if you have to but include something for each question. Remember that you will receive no credit for a blank and will probably receive some credit if you write something in answer to an essay question. If you guess a letter – say "B" for a multiple-choice question – you may have guessed right. If you leave a blank as an answer to a multiple-choice question, the examiners may respect your feelings but it will not add a point to your score. Some exams may penalize you for wrong answers, so in such cases *only*, you may not want to guess unless you have some basis for your answer.

7) Suggestions
    a. Objective-type questions
        1. Examine the question booklet for proper sequence of pages and questions
        2. Read all instructions carefully
        3. Skip any question which seems too difficult; return to it after all other questions have been answered
        4. Apportion your time properly; do not spend too much time on any single question or group of questions

5. Note and underline key words – *all, most, fewest, least, best, worst, same, opposite*, etc.
6. Pay particular attention to negatives
7. Note unusual option, e.g., unduly long, short, complex, different or similar in content to the body of the question
8. Observe the use of "hedging" words – *probably, may, most likely*, etc.
9. Make sure that your answer is put next to the same number as the question
10. Do not second-guess unless you have good reason to believe the second answer is definitely more correct
11. Cross out original answer if you decide another answer is more accurate; do not erase until you are ready to hand your paper in
12. Answer all questions; guess unless instructed otherwise
13. Leave time for review

  b. Essay questions
    1. Read each question carefully
    2. Determine exactly what is wanted. Underline key words or phrases.
    3. Decide on outline or paragraph answer
    4. Include many different points and elements unless asked to develop any one or two points or elements
    5. Show impartiality by giving pros and cons unless directed to select one side only
    6. Make and write down any assumptions you find necessary to answer the questions
    7. Watch your English, grammar, punctuation and choice of words
    8. Time your answers; don't crowd material

8) Answering the essay question

Most essay questions can be answered by framing the specific response around several key words or ideas. Here are a few such key words or ideas:

M's: manpower, materials, methods, money, management
P's: purpose, program, policy, plan, procedure, practice, problems, pitfalls, personnel, public relations

  a. Six basic steps in handling problems:
    1. Preliminary plan and background development
    2. Collect information, data and facts
    3. Analyze and interpret information, data and facts
    4. Analyze and develop solutions as well as make recommendations
    5. Prepare report and sell recommendations
    6. Install recommendations and follow up effectiveness

  b. Pitfalls to avoid
    1. *Taking things for granted* – A statement of the situation does not necessarily imply that each of the elements is necessarily true; for example, a complaint may be invalid and biased so that all that can be taken for granted is that a complaint has been registered

2. *Considering only one side of a situation* – Wherever possible, indicate several alternatives and then point out the reasons you selected the best one
3. *Failing to indicate follow up* – Whenever your answer indicates action on your part, make certain that you will take proper follow-up action to see how successful your recommendations, procedures or actions turn out to be
4. *Taking too long in answering any single question* – Remember to time your answers properly

IX. AFTER THE TEST

Scoring procedures differ in detail among civil service jurisdictions although the general principles are the same. Whether the papers are hand-scored or graded by machine we have described, they are nearly always graded by number. That is, the person who marks the paper knows only the number – never the name – of the applicant. Not until all the papers have been graded will they be matched with names. If other tests, such as training and experience or oral interview ratings have been given, scores will be combined. Different parts of the examination usually have different weights. For example, the written test might count 60 percent of the final grade, and a rating of training and experience 40 percent. In many jurisdictions, veterans will have a certain number of points added to their grades.

After the final grade has been determined, the names are placed in grade order and an eligible list is established. There are various methods for resolving ties between those who get the same final grade – probably the most common is to place first the name of the person whose application was received first. Job offers are made from the eligible list in the order the names appear on it. You will be notified of your grade and your rank as soon as all these computations have been made. This will be done as rapidly as possible.

People who are found to meet the requirements in the announcement are called "eligibles." Their names are put on a list of eligible candidates. An eligible's chances of getting a job depend on how high he stands on this list and how fast agencies are filling jobs from the list.

When a job is to be filled from a list of eligibles, the agency asks for the names of people on the list of eligibles for that job. When the civil service commission receives this request, it sends to the agency the names of the three people highest on this list. Or, if the job to be filled has specialized requirements, the office sends the agency the names of the top three persons who meet these requirements from the general list.

The appointing officer makes a choice from among the three people whose names were sent to him. If the selected person accepts the appointment, the names of the others are put back on the list to be considered for future openings.

That is the rule in hiring from all kinds of eligible lists, whether they are for typist, carpenter, chemist, or something else. For every vacancy, the appointing officer has his choice of any one of the top three eligibles on the list. This explains why the person whose name is on top of the list sometimes does not get an appointment when some of the persons lower on the list do. If the appointing officer chooses the second or third eligible, the No. 1 eligible does not get a job at once, but stays on the list until he is appointed or the list is terminated.

X. HOW TO PASS THE INTERVIEW TEST

The examination for which you applied requires an oral interview test. You have already taken the written test and you are now being called for the interview test – the final part of the formal examination.

You may think that it is not possible to prepare for an interview test and that there are no procedures to follow during an interview. Our purpose is to point out some things you can do in advance that will help you and some good rules to follow and pitfalls to avoid while you are being interviewed.

What is an interview supposed to test?

The written examination is designed to test the technical knowledge and competence of the candidate; the oral is designed to evaluate intangible qualities, not readily measured otherwise, and to establish a list showing the relative fitness of each candidate – as measured against his competitors – for the position sought. Scoring is not on the basis of "right" and "wrong," but on a sliding scale of values ranging from "not passable" to "outstanding." As a matter of fact, it is possible to achieve a relatively low score without a single "incorrect" answer because of evident weakness in the qualities being measured.

Occasionally, an examination may consist entirely of an oral test – either an individual or a group oral. In such cases, information is sought concerning the technical knowledges and abilities of the candidate, since there has been no written examination for this purpose. More commonly, however, an oral test is used to supplement a written examination.

Who conducts interviews?

The composition of oral boards varies among different jurisdictions. In nearly all, a representative of the personnel department serves as chairman. One of the members of the board may be a representative of the department in which the candidate would work. In some cases, "outside experts" are used, and, frequently, a businessman or some other representative of the general public is asked to serve. Labor and management or other special groups may be represented. The aim is to secure the services of experts in the appropriate field.

However the board is composed, it is a good idea (and not at all improper or unethical) to ascertain in advance of the interview who the members are and what groups they represent. When you are introduced to them, you will have some idea of their backgrounds and interests, and at least you will not stutter and stammer over their names.

What should be done before the interview?

While knowledge about the board members is useful and takes some of the surprise element out of the interview, there is other preparation which is more substantive. It *is* possible to prepare for an oral interview – in several ways:

1) Keep a copy of your application and review it carefully before the interview

This may be the only document before the oral board, and the starting point of the interview. Know what education and experience you have listed there, and the sequence and dates of all of it. Sometimes the board will ask you to review the highlights of your experience for them; you should not have to hem and haw doing it.

2) Study the class specification and the examination announcement

Usually, the oral board has one or both of these to guide them. The qualities, characteristics or knowledges required by the position sought are stated in these documents. They offer valuable clues as to the nature of the oral interview. For example, if the job involves supervisory responsibilities, the announcement will usually indicate that knowledge of modern supervisory methods and the qualifications of the candidate as a supervisor will be tested. If so, you can expect such questions, frequently in the form of a hypothetical situation which you are expected to solve. NEVER go into an oral without knowledge of the duties and responsibilities of the job you seek.

3) Think through each qualification required

Try to visualize the kind of questions you would ask if you were a board member. How well could you answer them? Try especially to appraise your own knowledge and background in each area, *measured against the job sought*, and identify any areas in which you are weak. Be critical and realistic – do not flatter yourself.

4) Do some general reading in areas in which you feel you may be weak

For example, if the job involves supervision and your past experience has NOT, some general reading in supervisory methods and practices, particularly in the field of human relations, might be useful. Do NOT study agency procedures or detailed manuals. The oral board will be testing your understanding and capacity, not your memory.

5) Get a good night's sleep and watch your general health and mental attitude

You will want a clear head at the interview. Take care of a cold or any other minor ailment, and of course, no hangovers.

What should be done on the day of the interview?

Now comes the day of the interview itself. Give yourself plenty of time to get there. Plan to arrive somewhat ahead of the scheduled time, particularly if your appointment is in the fore part of the day. If a previous candidate fails to appear, the board might be ready for you a bit early. By early afternoon an oral board is almost invariably behind schedule if there are many candidates, and you may have to wait. Take along a book or magazine to read, or your application to review, but leave any extraneous material in the waiting room when you go in for your interview. In any event, relax and compose yourself.

The matter of dress is important. The board is forming impressions about you – from your experience, your manners, your attitude, and your appearance. Give your personal appearance careful attention. Dress your best, but not your flashiest. Choose conservative, appropriate clothing, and be sure it is immaculate. This is a business interview, and your appearance should indicate that you regard it as such. Besides, being well groomed and properly dressed will help boost your confidence.

Sooner or later, someone will call your name and escort you into the interview room. *This is it.* From here on you are on your own. It is too late for any more preparation. But remember, you asked for this opportunity to prove your fitness, and you are here because your request was granted.

What happens when you go in?

The usual sequence of events will be as follows: The clerk (who is often the board stenographer) will introduce you to the chairman of the oral board, who will introduce you to the other members of the board. Acknowledge the introductions before you sit down. Do not be surprised if you find a microphone facing you or a stenotypist sitting by. Oral interviews are usually recorded in the event of an appeal or other review.

Usually the chairman of the board will open the interview by reviewing the highlights of your education and work experience from your application – primarily for the benefit of the other members of the board, as well as to get the material into the record. Do not interrupt or comment unless there is an error or significant misinterpretation; if that is the case, do not hesitate. But do not quibble about insignificant matters. Also, he will usually ask you some question about your education, experience or your present job – partly to get you to start talking and to establish the interviewing "rapport." He may start the actual questioning, or turn it over to one of the other members. Frequently, each member undertakes the questioning on a particular area, one in which he is perhaps most competent, so you can expect each member to participate in the examination. Because time is limited, you may also expect some rather abrupt switches in the direction the questioning takes, so do not be upset by it. Normally, a board member will not pursue a single line of questioning unless he discovers a particular strength or weakness.

After each member has participated, the chairman will usually ask whether any member has any further questions, then will ask you if you have anything you wish to add. Unless you are expecting this question, it may floor you. Worse, it may start you off on an extended, extemporaneous speech. The board is not usually seeking more information. The question is principally to offer you a last opportunity to present further qualifications or to indicate that you have nothing to add. So, if you feel that a significant qualification or characteristic has been overlooked, it is proper to point it out in a sentence or so. Do not compliment the board on the thoroughness of their examination – they have been sketchy, and you know it. If you wish, merely say, "No thank you, I have nothing further to add." This is a point where you can "talk yourself out" of a good impression or fail to present an important bit of information. Remember, *you close the interview yourself*.

The chairman will then say, "That is all, Mr. _____, thank you." Do not be startled; the interview is over, and quicker than you think. Thank him, gather your belongings and take your leave. Save your sigh of relief for the other side of the door.

How to put your best foot forward

Throughout this entire process, you may feel that the board individually and collectively is trying to pierce your defenses, seek out your hidden weaknesses and embarrass and confuse you. Actually, this is not true. They are obliged to make an appraisal of your qualifications for the job you are seeking, and they want to see you in your best light. Remember, they must interview all candidates and a non-cooperative candidate may become a failure in spite of their best efforts to bring out his qualifications. Here are 15 suggestions that will help you:

1) Be natural – Keep your attitude confident, not cocky

If you are not confident that you can do the job, do not expect the board to be. Do not apologize for your weaknesses, try to bring out your strong points. The board is interested in a positive, not negative, presentation. Cockiness will antagonize any board member and make him wonder if you are covering up a weakness by a false show of strength.

2) Get comfortable, but don't lounge or sprawl

Sit erectly but not stiffly. A careless posture may lead the board to conclude that you are careless in other things, or at least that you are not impressed by the importance of the occasion. Either conclusion is natural, even if incorrect. Do not fuss with your clothing, a pencil or an ashtray. Your hands may occasionally be useful to emphasize a point; do not let them become a point of distraction.

3) Do not wisecrack or make small talk

This is a serious situation, and your attitude should show that you consider it as such. Further, the time of the board is limited – they do not want to waste it, and neither should you.

4) Do not exaggerate your experience or abilities

In the first place, from information in the application or other interviews and sources, the board may know more about you than you think. Secondly, you probably will not get away with it. An experienced board is rather adept at spotting such a situation, so do not take the chance.

5) If you know a board member, do not make a point of it, yet do not hide it

Certainly you are not fooling him, and probably not the other members of the board. Do not try to take advantage of your acquaintanceship – it will probably do you little good.

6) Do not dominate the interview

Let the board do that. They will give you the clues – do not assume that you have to do all the talking. Realize that the board has a number of questions to ask you, and do not try to take up all the interview time by showing off your extensive knowledge of the answer to the first one.

7) Be attentive

You only have 20 minutes or so, and you should keep your attention at its sharpest throughout. When a member is addressing a problem or question to you, give him your undivided attention. Address your reply principally to him, but do not exclude the other board members.

8) Do not interrupt

A board member may be stating a problem for you to analyze. He will ask you a question when the time comes. Let him state the problem, and wait for the question.

9) Make sure you understand the question

Do not try to answer until you are sure what the question is. If it is not clear, restate it in your own words or ask the board member to clarify it for you. However, do not haggle about minor elements.

10) Reply promptly but not hastily

A common entry on oral board rating sheets is "candidate responded readily," or "candidate hesitated in replies." Respond as promptly and quickly as you can, but do not jump to a hasty, ill-considered answer.

11) Do not be peremptory in your answers

A brief answer is proper – but do not fire your answer back. That is a losing game from your point of view. The board member can probably ask questions much faster than you can answer them.

12) Do not try to create the answer you think the board member wants

He is interested in what kind of mind you have and how it works – not in playing games. Furthermore, he can usually spot this practice and will actually grade you down on it.

13) Do not switch sides in your reply merely to agree with a board member

Frequently, a member will take a contrary position merely to draw you out and to see if you are willing and able to defend your point of view. Do not start a debate, yet do not surrender a good position. If a position is worth taking, it is worth defending.

14) Do not be afraid to admit an error in judgment if you are shown to be wrong

The board knows that you are forced to reply without any opportunity for careful consideration. Your answer may be demonstrably wrong. If so, admit it and get on with the interview.

15) Do not dwell at length on your present job

The opening question may relate to your present assignment. Answer the question but do not go into an extended discussion. You are being examined for a *new* job, not your present one. As a matter of fact, try to phrase ALL your answers in terms of the job for which you are being examined.

Basis of Rating

Probably you will forget most of these "do's" and "don'ts" when you walk into the oral interview room. Even remembering them all will not ensure you a passing grade. Perhaps you did not have the qualifications in the first place. But remembering them will help you to put your best foot forward, without treading on the toes of the board members.

Rumor and popular opinion to the contrary notwithstanding, an oral board wants you to make the best appearance possible. They know you are under pressure – but they also want to see how you respond to it as a guide to what your reaction would be under the pressures of the job you seek. They will be influenced by the degree of poise you display, the personal traits you show and the manner in which you respond.

ABOUT THIS BOOK

This book contains tests divided into Examination Sections. Go through each test, answering every question in the margin. We have also attached a sample answer sheet at the back of the book that can be removed and used. At the end of each test look at the answer key and check your answers. On the ones you got wrong, look at the right answer choice and learn. Do not fill in the answers first. Do not memorize the questions and answers, but understand the answer and principles involved. On your test, the questions will likely be different from the samples. Questions are changed and new ones added. If you understand these past questions you should have success with any changes that arise. Tests may consist of several types of questions. We have additional books on each subject should more study be advisable or necessary for you. Finally, the more you study, the better prepared you will be. This book is intended to be the last thing you study before you walk into the examination room. Prior study of relevant texts is also recommended. NLC publishes some of these in our Fundamental Series. Knowledge and good sense are important factors in passing your exam. Good luck also helps. So now study this Passbook, absorb the material contained within and take that knowledge into the examination. Then do your best to pass that exam.

EXAMINATION SECTION

EXAMINATION SECTION
TEST 1

DIRECTIONS: Each question or incomplete statement is followed by several suggested answers or completions. Select the one that BEST answers the question or completes the statement. *PRINT THE LETTER OF THE CORRECT ANSWER IN THE SPACE AT THE RIGHT.*

1. A multi-line telephone with buttons for eight separate lines, plus a *hold* button, is often used when an office requires more than one outside line.
   If you are talking on one line of this type of office phone when another call comes in, what is the procedure to follow if you want to answer the second call but keep the first call on the line?
   Push the
   A. *hold* button at the same time as you push the *pickup* button of the ringing line
   B. *hold* button and then push the *pickup* button of the ringing line
   C. *pickup* button of the ringing line and then push the *hold* button
   D. *pickup* button of the ringing line and push the *hold* button when you return to the original line

2. Suppose that you are asked to prepare a petty cash statement for March. The original and one copy are to go to the personnel office. One copy is to go to the fiscal office, and another copy is to go to your supervisor. The last copy is for your files.
   In preparing the statement and the copies, how many sheets of copy paper should you use?
   A. 3   B. 4   C. 5   D. 8

3. Which one of the following is the LEAST important advantage of putting the subject of a letter in the heading to the right of the address? It
   A. makes filing of the copy easier
   B. makes more space available in the body of the letter
   C. simplifies distribution of letters
   D. simplifies determination of the subject of the letter

4. Of the following, the MOST efficient way to put 100 copies of a one-page letter into 9½" x 4⅛" envelopes for mailing is to fold _____ into an envelope.
   A. each letter and insert it immediately after folding
   B. each letter separately until all 100 are folded; then insert each one
   C. the 100 letters two at a time, then separate them and insert each one
   D. two letters together, slip them apart, and insert each one

5. When preparing papers for filing, it is NOT desirable to
   A. smooth papers that are wrinkled
   B. use paper clips to keep related papers together in the files
   C. arrange the papers in the order in which they will be filed
   D. mend torn papers with cellophane tape

6. Of the following, the BEST reason for a clerical unit to have its own duplicating machine is that the unit
   A. uses many forms which it must reproduce internally
   B. must make two copies of each piece of incoming mail for a special file
   C. must make seven copies of each piece of outgoing mail
   D. must type 200 envelopes each month for distribution to the same offices

7. Several offices use the same photocopying machine.
   If each office must pay its share of the cost of running this machine, the BEST way of determining how much of this cost should be charged to each of these offices is to
   A. determine the monthly number of photocopies made by each office
   B. determine the monthly number of originals submitted for photocopying by each office
   C. determine the number of times per day each office uses the photocopying machine
   D. divide the total cost of running the photocopy machine by the total number of offices using the machine

8. Which one of the following would it be BEST to use to indicate that a file folder has been removed from the files for temporary use in another office?
   A(n)
   A. cross-reference card   B. tickler file marker
   C. aperture card   D. out guide

9. Which one of the following is the MOST important objective of filing?
   A. Giving a secretary something to do in her spare time
   B. Making it possible to locate information quickly
   C. Providing a place to store unneeded documents
   D. Keeping extra papers from accumulating on workers' desks

10. If a check has been made out for an incorrect amount, the BEST action for the writer of the check to take is to
    A. erase the original amount and enter the correct amount
    B. cross out the original amount with a single line and enter the correct amount above it
    C. black out the original amount so that it cannot be read and enter the correct amount above it
    D. write a new check

11. Which one of the following BEST describes the usual arrangement of a tickler file?
    A. Alphabetical
    B. Chronological
    C. Numerical
    D. Geographical

12. Which one of the following is the LEAST desirable filing practice?
    A. Using staples to keep papers together
    B. Filing all material without regard to date
    C. Keeping a record of all materials removed from the files
    D. Writing filing instructions on each paper prior to filing

13. Assume that one of your duties is to keep records of the office supplies used by your unit for the purpose of ordering new supplies when the old supplies run out.
    The information that will be of MOST help in letting you know when to reorder supplies is the
    A. quantity issued
    B. quantity received
    C. quantity on hand
    D. stock number

Questions 14-19.

DIRECTIONS: Questions 14 through 19 consist of sets of names and addresses. In each question, the name and address in Column II should be an exact copy of the name and address in Column I. If there is
    a mistake *only* in the name, mark your answer A;
    a mistake *only* in the address, mark your answer B;
    a mistake in *both* name and address, mark your answer C;
    no mistake in either name or address, mark your answer D.

SAMPLE QUESTION

Column I
Michael Filbert
456 Reade Street
New York, N.Y. 10013

Column II
Michael Filbert
645 Reade Street
New York, N.Y. 10013

Since there is a mistake only in the address (the street number should be 456 instead of 645), the answer to the sample question is B.

COLUMN I

COLUMN II

14. Esta Wong
    141 West 68 St.
    New York, N.Y. 10023

    Esta Wang
    141 West 68 St.
    New York,, N.Y. 10023

15. Dr. Alberto Grosso
    3475 12th Avenue
    Brooklyn, N.Y. 11218

    Dr. Alberto Grosso
    3475 12th Avenue
    Brooklyn, N.Y. 11218

	Column I	Column II	

16. Mrs. Ruth Bortlas
482 Theresa Ct.
Far Rockaway, N.Y. 11691

    Ms. Ruth Bortlas
482 Theresa Ct.
Far Rockaway, N.Y. 11169

    16.____

17. Mr. and Mrs. Howard Fox
2301 Sedgwick Avenue
Bronx, N.Y. 10468

    Mr. and Mrs. Howard Fox
231 Sedgwick Ave.
Bronx, N.Y. 10458

    17.____

18. Miss Marjorie Black
223 East 23 Street
New York, N.Y. 10010

    Miss Margorie Black
223 East 23 Street
New York, N.Y. 10010

    18.____

19. Michelle Herman
806 Valley Rd.
Old Tappan, N.J. 07675

    Michelle Hermann
806 Valley Dr.
Old Tappan, N.J. 07675

    19.____

Questions 20-25.

DIRECTIONS: Questions 20 through 25 are to be answered SOLELY on the basis of the information in the following passage.

Basic to every office is the need for proper lighting. Inadequate lighting is a familiar cause of fatigue and serves to create a somewhat dismal atmosphere in the office. One requirement of proper lighting is that it be of an appropriate intensity. Intensity is measured in foot-candles. According to the Illuminating Engineering Society of New York, for casual seeing tasks such as in reception rooms, inactive file rooms, and other service areas, it is recommended that the amount of light be 30 foot-candles. For ordinary seeing tasks such as reading and work in active file rooms and in mail rooms, the recommended lighting is 100 foot-candles. For very difficult seeing tasks such as accounting, transcribing, and business machine use, the recommended lighting is 150 foot-candles.

Lighting intensity is only one requirement. Shadows and glare are to be avoided. For example, the larger the proportion of a ceiling filled with lighting units, the more glare-free and comfortable the lighting will be. Natural lighting from windows is not too dependable because on dark wintry days, windows yield little usable light, and on sunny afternoons, the glare from windows may be very distracting. Desks should not face the windows. Finally, the main lighting source ought to be overhead and to the left of the user.

20. According to the above passage, insufficient light in the office may cause 20.____
    A. glare   B. shadows   C. tiredness   D. distraction

21. Based on the above passage, which of the following must be considered when planning lighting arrangements? 21.____
    The
    A. amount of natural light present
    B. amount of work to be done
    C. level of difficulty of work to be done
    D. type of activity to be carried out

22. It can be inferred from the above passage that a well-coordinated lighting scheme is LIKELY to result in
    A. greater employee productivity
    B. elimination of light reflection
    C. lower lighting cost
    D. more use of natural light

23. Of the following, the BEST title for the above passage is
    A. Characteristics of Light
    B. Light Measurement Devices
    C. Factors to Consider When Planning Lighting Systems
    D. Comfort vs. Cost When Devising Lighting Arrangements

24. According to the above passage, a foot-candle is a measurement of the
    A. number of bulbs used
    B. strength of the light
    C. contrast between glare and shadow
    D. proportion of the ceiling filled with lighting units

25. According to the above passage, the number of foot-candles of light that would be needed to copy figures onto a payroll is _____ foot-candles.
    A. less than 30   B. 30   C. 100   D. 150

KEY (CORRECT ANSWERS)

1.	B		11.	B
2.	B		12.	B
3.	B		13.	C
4.	A		14.	A
5.	B		15.	D
6.	A		16.	C
7.	A		17.	B
8.	D		18.	A
9.	B		19.	C
10.	D		20.	C

21. D
22. A
23. C
24. B
25. D

TEST 2

DIRECTIONS: Each question or incomplete statement is followed by several suggested answers or completions. Select the one that BEST answers the question or completes the statement. *PRINT THE LETTER OF THE CORRECT ANSWER IN THE SPACE AT THE RIGHT.*

1. Assume that a supervisor has three subordinates who perform clerical tasks. One of the employees retires and is replaced by someone who is transferred from another unit in the agency. The transferred employee tells the supervisor that she has worked as a clerical employee for two years and understands clerical operations quite well. The supervisor then assigns the transferred employee to a desk, tells the employee to begin working, and returns to his own desk.
The supervisor's action in this situation is
    A. *proper;* experienced clerical employees do not require training when they are transferred to new assignments
    B. *improper;* before the supervisor returns to his desk, he should tell the other two subordinates to watch the transferred employee perform the work
    C. *proper;* if the transferred employee makes any mistakes, she will bring them to the supervisor's attention
    D. *improper;* the supervisor should find out what clerical tasks the transferred employee has performed and give her instruction in those which are new or different

1.____

2. Assume that you are falling behind in completing your work assignments and you believe that your workload is too heavy.
Of the following, the BEST course of action for you to take FIRST is to
    A. discuss the problem with your supervisor
    B. decide which of your assignments can be postponed
    C. try to get some of your co-workers to help you out
    D. plan to take some of the work home with you in order to catch up

2.____

3. Suppose that one of the clerks under your supervision is filling in monthly personnel forms. She asks you to explain a particular personnel regulation which is related to various items on the forms. You are not thoroughly familiar with the regulation.
Of the following responses you may make, the one which will gain the MOST respect from the clerk and which is generally the MOST advisable is to
    A. tell the clerk to do the best she can and that you will check her work later
    B. inform the clerk that you are not sure of a correct explanation but suggest a procedure for her to follow
    C. give the clerk a suitable interpretation so that she will think you are familiar with all regulations
    D. tell the clerk that you will have to read the regulation more thoroughly before you can give her an explanation

3.____

4. Charging out records until a specified due date, with prompt follow-up if they are not returned, is a   4._____
   A. *good* idea; it may prevent the records from being kept needlessly on someone's desk for long periods of time
   B. *good* idea; it will indicate the extent of your authority to other departments
   C. *poor* idea; the person borrowing the material may make an error because of the pressure put upon him to return the records
   D. *poor* idea; other departments will feel that you do not trust them with the records and they will be resentful

Questions 5-9.

DIRECTIONS: Questions 5 through 9 consist of three lines of code letters and numbers. The numbers on each line should correspond with the code letters on the same line in accordance with the table below.

Code Letter	P	L	I	J	B	O	H	U	C	G
Corresponding Letter	0	1	2	3	4	5	6	7	8	9

On some of the lines, an error exists in the coding. Compare the letters and numbers in each question carefully. If you find an error or errors on
  only one of the lines in the question, mark your answer A;
  any two lines in the question, mark your answer B;
  all three lines in the question, mark your answer C;
  none of the lines in the question, mark your answer D.

SAMPLE QUESTION
JHOILCP   3652180
BICLGUP   4286970
UCIBHLJ   5824613

In the above sample, the first line is correct since each code letter listed has the correct corresponding number. On the second line, an error exists because code letter L should have the number 1 instead of the number 6. On the third line, an error exists because the code letter U should have the number 7 instead of the number 5. Since there are errors on two of the three lines, the correct answer is B.

5. BULJCIP   4713920   5._____
    HIGPOUL   6290571
    OCUHJJBI   5876342

6. CUBLOIJ   8741023   6._____
    LCLGCLB   1818914
    JPUHIOC   3076158

7. OIJGCBPO   52398405   7._____
    UHPBLIOP   76041250
    CLUIPGPC   81720908

8. BPCOUOJI   40875732
    UOHCIPLB   75682014
    GLHUUCBJ   92677843

9. HOIOHJLH   65256361
    IOJJHHBP   25536640
    OJHBJOPI   53642502

Questions 10-13.

DIRECTIONS: Questions 10 through 13 are to be answered SOLELY on the basis of the information given in the following passage.

The mental attitude of the employee toward safety is exceedingly important in preventing accidents. All efforts designed to keep safety on the employee's mind and to keep accident prevention a live subject in the office will help substantially in a safety program. Although it may seem strange, it is common for people to be careless. Therefore, safety education is a continuous process.

Safety rules should be explained, and the reasons for their rigid enforcement should be given to employees. Telling employees to be careful or giving similar general safety warnings and slogans is probably of little value. Employees should be informed of basic safety fundamentals. This can be done through staff meetings, informal suggestions to employees, movies, and safety instruction cards. Safety instruction cards provide the employees with specific suggestions about safety and serve as a series of timely reminder helping to keep safety on the minds of employees. Pictures, posters, and cartoon sketches on bulletin boards that are located in areas continually used by employees arouse the employees' interest in safety. It is usually good to supplement this type of safety promotion with intensive individual follow-up.

10. The above passage implies that the LEAST effective of the following safety measures is
    A. rigid enforcement of safety rules
    B. getting employees to think in terms of safety
    C. elimination of unsafe conditions in the office
    D. telling employees to stay alert at all times

11. The reason given by the passage for maintaining ongoing safety education is that
    A. people are often careless
    B. office tasks are often dangerous
    C. the value of safety slogans increases with repetition
    D. safety rules change frequently

12. Which one of the following safety aids is MOST likely to be preferred by the passage? A
    A. cartoon of a man tripping over a carton and yelling, *Keep aisles clear!*
    B. poster with a large number one and a caption saying, *Safety First*

C. photograph of a very neatly arranged office
D. large sign with the word THINK in capital letters

13. Of the following, the BEST title for the above passage is 13.____
    A. Basic Safety Fundamentals
    B. Enforcing Safety Among Careless Employees
    C. Attitudes Toward Safety
    D. Making Employees Aware of Safety

Questions 14-21.

DIRECTIONS: Questions 14 through 21 are to be answered SOLELY on the basis of the information and chart given below.

The following chart shows expenses in five selected categories for a one-year period, expressed as percentages of these same expenses during the previous year. The chart compares two different offices. In Office T (represented by ▓▓▓▓), a cost reduction program has been tested for the past year. The other office, Office Q (represented by ////), served as a control, in that no special effort was made to reduce costs during the past year.

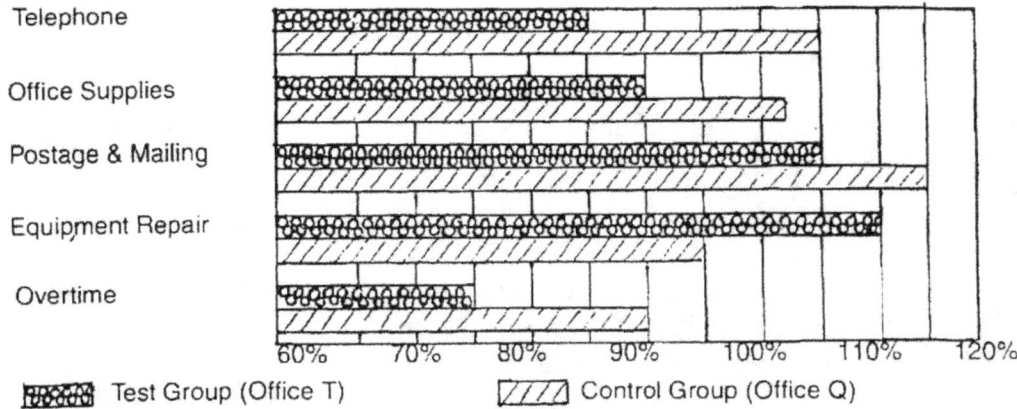

RESULTS OF OFFICE COST REDUCTION PROGRAM
Expenses of Test and Control Groups for 2020
Expressed as Percentages of Same Expenses for 2019

14. In Office T, which category of expense showed the greatest percentage REDUCTION from 2019 to 2020? 14.____
    A. Telephone   B. Office Supplies
    C. Postage & Mailing   D. Overtime

15. In which expense category did Office T show the BEST results in percentage terms when compared to Office Q? 15.____
    A. Telephone   B. Office Supplies
    C. Postage & Mailing   D. Overtime

16. According to the above chart, the cost reduction program was LEAST effective for the expense category of
    A. Office Supplies
    B. Postage & Mailing
    C. Equipment Repair
    D. Overtime

17. Office T's telephone costs went down during 2020 by approximately how many percentage points?
    A. 15
    B. 20
    C. 85
    D. 104

18. Which of the following changes occurred in expenses for Office Supplies in Office Q in the year 2020 as compared with the year 2019?
    They
    A. increased by more than 100%
    B. remained the same
    C. decreased by a few percentage points
    D. increased by a few percentage points

19. For which of the following expense categories do the results in Office T and the results in Office Q differ MOST NEARLYY by 10 percentage points?
    A. Telephone
    B. Postage & Mailing
    C. Equipment Repair
    D. Overtime

20. In which expense category did Office Q's costs show the GREATEST percentage increase in 2020?
    A. Telephone
    B. Office Supplies
    C. Postage & Mailing
    D. Equipment Repair

21. In Office T, by approximately what percentage did overtime expense change during the past year? It
    A. *increased* by 15%
    B. *increased* by 75%
    C. *decreased* by 10%
    D. *decreased* by 25%

22. In a particular agency, there were 160 accidents in 2017. Of these accidents, 75% were due to unsafe acts and the rest were due to unsafe conditions. In the following year, a special safety program was established. The number of accidents in 2019 due to unsafe acts was reduced to 35% of what it had been in 2017.
    How many accidents due to unsafe acts were there in 2019?
    A. 20
    B. 36
    C. 42
    D. 56

23. At the end of every month, the petty cash fund of Agency A is reimbursed for payments made from the fund during the month. During the month of February, the amounts paid from the fund were entered on receipts as follows: 10 bus fares of $3.50 each and one taxi fare of $35.00. At the end of the month, the money left in the fund was in the following denominations: 15 ten-dollar bills, 10 one-dollar bills, 40 quarters, and 100 dimes.
    If the petty cash fund is reduced by 20% for the following month, how much money will there be available in the petty cash fund for March?
    A. $110.00
    B. $200.00
    C. $215.00
    D. $250.00

24. The one of the following records which it would be MOST advisable to keep in alphabetical order is a
    A. continuous listing of phone messages, including time and caller, for your supervisor
    B. listing of individuals currently employed by your agency in a particular title
    C. record of purchases paid for by the petty cash fund
    D. dated record of employees who have borrowed material from the files in your office

25. Assume that you have been asked to copy by hand a column of numbers with two decimal places from one record to another. Each number consists of three, four, and five digits.
    In order to copy them quickly and accurately, you should copy
    A. each number exactly, making sure that the column of digits farthest to the right is in a straight line and all other columns are lined up
    B. the column of digits farthest to the right and then copy the next column of digits moving from right to left
    C. the column of digits farthest to the left and then copy the next column of digits moving from left to right
    D. the digits to the right of each decimal point and then copy the digits to the left of each decimal point

KEY (CORRECT ANSWERS)

1.	D		11.	A
2.	A		12.	A
3.	D		13.	D
4.	A		14.	D
5.	A		15.	A
6.	C		16.	C
7.	D		17.	A
8.	B		18.	D
9.	C		19.	B
10.	D		20.	C

21. D
22. C
23. B
24. B
25. A

EXAMINATION SECTION
TEST 1

DIRECTIONS: Each question or incomplete statement is followed by several suggested answers or completions. Select the one that BEST answers the question or completes the statement. *PRINT THE LETTER OF THE CORRECT ANSWER IN THE SPACE AT THE RIGHT.*

Questions 1-2.

DIRECTIONS: Questions 1 and 2 are to be answered on the basis of the following conditions.

Assume that you work for Department A, which occupies several floors in one building. There is a reception office on each floor. All visitors (persons not employed in the department) are required to go to the reception office on the same floor as the office of the person they want to see. They sign a register, their presence is announced by the receptionist, and they wait in the reception room for the person they are visiting.

1. As you are walking in the corridor of your department on your way to a meeting in Room 314, a visitor approaches you and asks you to direct her to Room 312. She says that she is delivering some papers to Mr. Crane in that office. The MOST APPROPRIATE action for you to take is to

    A. offer to deliver the papers to Mr. Crane since you will be passing his office
    B. suggest that she come with you since you will be passing Room 312
    C. direct her to the reception office where Mr. Crane will be contacted for her
    D. take her to the reception office and contact Mr. Crane for her

1.____

2. You are acting as receptionist in the reception office on the second floor. A man enters, stating that he is an accountant from another department and that he has an appointment with Mr. Prince, who is located in Room 102 on the first floor.
The BEST action for you to take is to

    A. phone the reception office on the first floor and ask the receptionist to contact Mr. Prince
    B. advise the man to go to the reception office on the first floor where he will be further assisted
    C. contact Mr. Prince for him and ask that he come to your office where his visitor is waiting
    D. send him directly to Room 102 where he can see Mr. Prince

2.____

3. One of the employees whom you supervise complains to you that you give her more work than the other employees and that she cannot finish these assignments by the time you expect them to be completed.
Of the following, the FIRST action you should then take is to

    A. tell the employee that you expect more work from her because the other employees do not have her capabilities
    B. assure the employee that you always divide the work equally among your subordinates

3.____

13

C. review the employee's recent assignments in order to determine whether her complaint is justified
D. ask the employee if there are any personal problems which are interfering with the completion of the assignments

4. Assume that a staff regulation exists which requires an employee to inform his supervisor if the employee will be absent on a particular day.
If an employee fails to follow this regulation, the FIRST action his supervisor should take is to

   A. inform his own supervisor of the situation and ask for further instructions
   B. ask the employee to explain his failure to follow the regulation
   C. tell the employee that another breach of the regulation will lead to disciplinary action
   D. reprimand the employee for failing to follow the regulation

4.____

5. An employee tells his supervisor that he submitted an idea to the employees' suggestion program by mail over two months ago and still has not received an indication that the suggestion is being considered. The employee states that when one of his co-workers sent in a suggestion, he received a response within one week. The employee then asks his supervisor what he should do.
Which of the following is the BEST response for the supervisor to make?

   A. "Next time you have a suggestion, see me about it first and I will make sure that it is properly handled."
   B. "I'll try to find out whether your suggestion was received by the program and whether a response was sent."
   C. "Your suggestion probably wasn't that good so there's no sense in pursuing the matter any further."
   D. "Let's get together and submit the suggestion jointly so that it will carry more weight."

5.____

6. Assume that you have been trying to teach a newly appointed employee the filing procedures used in your office. The employee seems to be having difficulty learning the procedures even though you consider them relatively simple and you originally learned them in less time than you have already spent trying to teach the new employee.
Before you spend any time trying to teach him any new filing procedures, which of the following actions should you take FIRST?

   A. Try to teach him some other aspect of your office's work.
   B. Tell him that you had little difficulty learning the procedures and ask him why he finds them so hard to learn.
   C. Review with him those procedures you have tried to teach him and determine whether he understands them.
   D. Report to your supervisor that the new employee is unsuited for the work performed in your office.

6.____

7. There is a rule in your office that all employees must sign in and out for lunch. You notice that a new employee who is under your direct supervision has not signed in or out for lunch for the past three days. Of the following, the MOST effective action to take is to

7.____

A. immediately report this matter to your supervisor
B. note this infraction of rules on the employee's personnel record
C. remind the employee that she must sign in and out for lunch every day
D. send around a memorandum to all employees in the office telling them they must sign in and out for lunch every day

Questions 8-15.

DIRECTIONS: Questions 8 through 15 each show in Column I names written on four cards (lettered w, x, y, z) which have to be filed. You are to choose the option (lettered A, B, C, or D) in Column II which BEST represents the proper order of filing according to the rules and sample question given below. The cards are to be filed according to the following Rules for Alphabetical Filing.

RULES FOR ALPHABETICAL FILING

Names of Individuals

1. The names of individuals are filed in strict alphabetical order, first according to the last name, then according to first name or initial, and finally according to middle name or initial. For example: George Allen precedes Edward Bell and Leonard Reston precedes Lucille Reston.

2. When last names are the same, for example, A. Green and Agnes Green, the one with the initial comes before the one with the name written out when the first initials are identical.

3. When first and last names are the same, a name without a middle initial comes before one with a middle initial. For example: Ralph Simon comes before both Ralph A. Simon and Ralph Adam Simon.

4. When first and last names are the same, a name with a middle initial comes before one with a middle name beginning with the same initial. For example: Sam P. Rogers comes before Sam Paul Rogers.

5. Prefixes such as De , 0', Mac, Mc, and Van are filed as written and are treated as part of the names to which they are connected. For example: Gladys McTeaque is filed before Frances Meadows.

6. Abbreviated names are treated as if they were spelled out. For example: Chas. is filed as Charles and Thos. is filed as Thomas.

7. Titles and designations such as Dr., Mr., and Prof, are ignored in filing.

Names of Organizations

1. The names of business organizations are filed according to the order in which each word in the name appears. When an organization name bears the name of a person, it is filed according to the rules for filing names of people as given above. Vivian Quinn Boutique would, therefore, come before Security Locks Inc. because Quinn comes before Security.

4 (#1)

2. *When numerals occur in a name, they are treated as if they were spelled out. For example: 4th Street Thrift Shop is filed as Fourth Street Thrift Shop.*

3. *When the following words are part of the name of an organization, they are ignored: on, the, of, and.*

SAMPLE

	Column I	Column II	The correct way to file the cards is:
w.	Jane Earl	A. w, y, z, x	y. James Earl
x.	James A. Earle	B. y, w, z, x	w. Jane Earl
y.	James Earl	C. x, y, w, z	z. J. Earle
z.	J. Earle	D. x, w, y, z	x. James A. Earle

The correct filing order is shown by the letters, y, w, z, x (in that sequence). Since, in Column II, B appears in front of the letters, y, w, z, x (in that sequence), B is the correct answer to the sample question.

Now answer the following questions using that same procedure.

Column I

8. w. James Rothschild
    x. Julius B. Rothchild
    y. B. Rothstein
    z. Brian Joel Rothenstein

Column II

A. x, z, w, y
B. x, w, z, y
C. z, y, w, x
D. z, w, x, y

8.____

9. w. George S. Wise
    x. S. G. Wise
    y. Geo. Stuart Wise
    z. Prof. Diana Wise

A. w, y, z, x
B. x, w, y, z
C. y, x, w, z
D. z, w, y, x

9.____

10. w. 10th Street Bus Terminal
    x. Buckingham Travel Agency
    y. The Buckingham Theater
    z. Burt Tompkins Studio

A. x, z, w, y
B. y, x, w, z
C. w, z, y, x
D. x, w, y, z

10.____

11. w. National Council of American Importers
    x. National Chain Co. of Providence
    y. National Council on Alcoholism
    z. National Chain Co.

A. w, y, x, z
B. x, z, w, y
C. z, x, w, y
D. z, x, y, w

11.____

12. w. Dr. Herbert Alvary
    x. Mr. Victor Alvarado
    y. Alvar Industries
    z. V. Alvarado

A. w, y, x, z
B. z, w, x, y
C. y, z, x, w
D. w, z, x, y

12.____

	Column I		Column II
13.	w. Joan MacBride x. Wm. Mackey y. Roslyn McKenzie z. Winifred Mackey		A. w, x, z, y B. w, y, z, x C. w, z, x, y D. w, y, x, z	13._____

	Column I		Column II
14.	w. 3 Way Trucking Co. x. 3rd Street Bakery y. 380 Realty Corp. z. Three Lions Pub		A. y, x, z, w B. y, z, w, x C. x, y, z, w D. x, y, w, z	14._____
15.	w. Miss Rose Leonard x. Rev. Leonard Lucas y. Sylvia Leonard Linen Shop z. Rose S. Leonard		A. z, w, x, y B. w, z, y, x C. w, x, z, y D. z, w, y, x	15._____

Questions 16-19.

DIRECTIONS: Answer Questions 16 through 19 ONLY on the basis of the information given in the following passage.

Work measurement concerns accomplishment or productivity. It has to do with results; it does not deal with the amount of energy used up, although in many cases this may be in direct proportion to the work output. Work measurement not only helps a manager to distribute work loads fairly, but it also enables him to define work sueeess in actual units, evaluate employee performance, and determine where corrective help is needed. Work measurement is accomplished by measuring the amount produced, measuring the time spent to produce it, and relating the two. To illustrate, it is common to speak of so many orders processed within a given time. The number of orders processed becomes meaningful when related to the amount of time taken.

Much of the work in an office can be measured fairly accurately and inexpensively. The extent of wo.rk measurement possible in any given case will depend upon the particular type of office tasks performed, but usually from two-thirds to three-fourths of all work in an office can be measured. It is true that difficulty in work measurement is encountered, for example, when the office work is irregular and not repeated often, or when the work is primarily mental rather than manual. These are problems, but they are used as excuses for doing no work measurement far more frequently than is justified.

16. According to the above passage, which of the following BEST illustrates the type of information obtained as a result of work measurement? A 16._____

    A. clerk takes one hour to file 150 folders
    B. typist types five letters
    C. stenographer works harder typing from shorthand notes than she does typing from a typed draft
    D. clerk keeps track of employees' time by computing sick leave, annual leave, and overtime leave

17. The above passage does NOT indicate that work measurement can be used to help a supervisor to determine
    A. why an employee is performing poorly on the job
    B. who are the fast and slow workers in the unit
    C. how the work in the unit should be divided up
    D. how long it should take to perform a certain task

18. According to the above passage, the kind of work that would be MOST difficult to measure would be such work as
    A. sorting mail
    B. designing a form for a new procedure
    C. photocopying various materials
    D. answering inquiries with form letters

19. The excuses mentioned in the above passage for failure to perform work measurement can be BEST summarized as the
    A. repetitive nature of office work
    B. costs involved in carrying out accurate work measurement
    C. inability to properly use the results obtained from work measurement
    D. difficulty involved in measuring certain types of work

Questions 20-24.

DIRECTIONS: In each of Questions 20 through 24, there is a sentence containing one underlined word. Choose the word (lettered A, B, C, or D) which means MOST NEARLY the same as the underlined word as it is used in the sentence.

20. Mr. Warren could not attend the luncheon because he had a prior appointment.
    A. conflicting   B. official
    C. previous   D. important

21. The time allowed to complete the task was not adequate.
    A. long   B. enough   C. excessive   D. required

22. The investigation unit began an extensive search for the information.
    A. complicated   B. superficial
    C. thorough   D. leisurely

23. The secretary answered the telephone in a courteous manner.
    A. businesslike   B. friendly
    C. formal   D. polite

24. The recipient of the money checked the total amount.
    A. receiver   B. carrier   C. borrower   D. giver

25. You receive a telephone call from an employee in another agency requesting information about a project being carried out by a division other than your own. You know little about the work being done, but you would like to help the caller.
   Of the following, the BEST action for you to take is to
   A. ask the caller exactly what he would like to know and then tell him all you know about the work being done
   B. ask the caller to tell you exactly what he would like to know so that you can get the information while he waits
   C. tell the caller that you will have the call transferred to the division working on the project
   D. request that the caller write to you so that you can send him the necessary information

---

KEY (CORRECT ANSWERS)

1. C
2. B
3. C
4. B
5. B

6. C
7. C
8. A
9. D
10. B

11. D
12. C
13. A
14. C
15. B

16. A
17. A
18. B
19. D
20. C

21. B
22. C
23. D
24. A
25. C

TEST 2

DIRECTIONS: Each question or incomplete statement is followed by several suggested answers or completions. Select the one that BEST answers the question or completes the statement. *PRINT THE LETTER OF THE CORRECT ANSWER IN THE SPACE AT THE RIGHT.*

1. Which of the following actions by a supervisor is LEAST likely to result in an increase in morale or productivity?   1.___

   A. Delegating additional responsibility but not authority to his subordinates
   B. Spending more time than his subordinates in planning and organizing the office's work
   C. Giving positive rather than negative orders to his subordinates
   D. Keeping his subordinates informed about changes in rules or policies which affect their work

Questions 2-8.

DIRECTIONS: Questions 2 through 8 are based SOLELY on the information and the form given below.

The following form is a Weekly Summary of New Employees and lists all employees appointed to Department F in the week indicated. In addition to the starting date and name, the form includes each new employee's time card number, title, status, work location and supervisor's name.

DEPARTMENT F						
Weekly Summary of New Employees					Week Starting March 25	
Starting Date	Name Last, First	Time Card No.	Title	Status	Work Location	Supervisor
3/25	Astaire, Hannah	361	Typist	Prov.	Rm. 312	Merrill, Judy
3/25	Silber, Arthur	545	Clerk	Perm.	Rm. 532	Rizzo, Joe
3/26	Vecchio, Robert	620	Accountant	Perm.	Rm. 620	Harper, Ruth
3/26	Goldberg, Sally	373	Stenographer	Prov.	Rm. 308	Merrill, Judy
3/26	Yee, Bruce	555	Accountant	Perm.	Rm. 530	Rizzo, Joe
3/27	Dunning, Betty	469	Typist	Perm.	Rm. 411	Miller, Tony
3/28	Goldman, Sara	576	Stenographer	Prov.	Rm. 532	Rizzo, Joe
3/29	Vesquez, Roy	624	Accountant	Perm.	Rm. 622	Harper, Ruth
3/29	Browning, David	464	Typist	Perm.	Rm. 411	Miller, Tony

2. On which one of the following dates did two employees *in the same title* begin work?   2.____

   A. 3/25   B. 3/26   C. 3/27   D. 3/29

3. To which one of the following supervisors was ONE typist assigned?   3.____

   A. Judy Merrill   B. Tony Miller
   C. Ruth Harper   D. Joe Rizzo

4. Which one of the following supervisors was assigned the GREATEST number of new employees during the week of March 25?   4.____

   A. Ruth Harper   B. Judy Merrill
   C. Tony Miller   D. Joe Rizzo

5. Which one of the following employees was assigned *three days after another employee* to the same job location?   5.____

   A. Sara Goldman   B. David Browning
   C. Bruce Yee   D. Roy Vesquez

6. The title in which BOTH provisional and permanent appointments were made is   6.____

   A. accountant   B. clerk   C. stenographer   D. typist

7. The employee who started work on the SAME day and have the SAME status but DIFFERENT titles are   7.____

   A. Arthur Silber and Hannah Astaire
   B. Robert Vecchio and Bruce Yee
   C. Sally Goldberg and Sara Goldman
   D. Roy Vesquez and David Browning

8. On the basis of the information given on the form, which one of the following conclusions regarding time card numbers appears to be CORRECT?   8.____

   A. The first digit of the time card number is coded according to the assigned title.
   B. The middle digit of the time card number is coded according to the assigned title.
   C. The first digit of the time card number is coded according to the employees' floor locations.
   D. Time card numbers are randomly assigned.

9. Assume that a caller arrives at your desk and states that she is your supervisor's daughter and that she would like to see her father. You have been under the impression that your supervisor has only a two-year-old son.
   Of the following, the BEST way to deal with this visitor is to   9.____

   A. offer her a seat and advise your supervisor of the visitor
   B. tell her to go right in to her father's office
   C. ask her for some proof to show that she is your supervisor's daughter
   D. escort her into your supervisor's office and ask him if the visitor is his daughter

10. Assume that you answer the telephone and the caller says that he is a police officer and asks for personal information about one of your co-workers.
    Of the following, the BEST course of action for you to take is to   10.____

A. give the caller the information he has requested
B. ask the caller for the telephone number of the phone he is using, call him back, and then give him the information
C. refuse to give him any information and offer to transfer the call to your supervisor
D. ask the caller for his name and badge number before giving him the information

Questions 11-16.

DIRECTIONS: Questions 11 through 16 each consist of a sentence which may or may not be an example of good English usage. Consider grammar, punctuation, spelling, capitalization, awkwardness, etc. Examine each sentence, and then choose the correct statement about it from the four choices below it. If the English usage in the sentence given is better than it would be with any of the changes suggested in Options B, C, or D, choose Option A. Do not choose an option that will change the meaning of the sentence.

11. The recruiting officer said, *"There are many different goverment jobs available."*   11.____

    A. This is an example of acceptable writing.
    B. The word *There* should not be capitalized.
    C. The word *goverment* should be spelled *government.*
    D. The comma after the word *said* should be removed.

12. He can recommend a mechanic whose work is reliable.   12.____

    A. This is an example of acceptable writing.
    B. The word *reliable* should be spelled *relyable.*
    C. The word *whose* should be spelled *who's.*
    D. The word *mechanic* should be spelled *mecanic.*

13. She typed quickly; like someone who had not a moment to lose.   13.____

    A. This is an example of acceptable writing.
    B. The word *not* should be removed.
    C. The semicolon should be changed to a comma.
    D. The word *quickly* should be placed before instead of after the word *typed.*

14. She insisted that she had to much work to do.   14.____

    A. This is an example of acceptable writing.
    B. The word *insisted* should be spelled *incisted.*
    C. The word *to* used in front of *much* should be spelled *too.*
    D. The word *do* should be changed to *be done.*

15. He excepted praise from his supervisor for a job well done.   15.____

    A. This is an example of acceptable writing.
    B. The word *excepted* should be spelled *accepted.*
    C. The order of the words *well done* should be changed to *done well.*
    D. There should be a comma after the word, *supervisor*

16. What appears to be intentional errors in grammar occur several times in the passage.

    A. This is an example of acceptable writing.
    B. The word *occur* should be spelled *occurr*.
    C. The word *appears* should be changed to *appear*.
    D. The phrase *several times* should be changed to *from time to time*.

17. The daily compensation to be paid to each consultant hired in a certain agency is computed by dividing his professional earnings in the previous year by 250. The maximum daily compensation they can receive is $200 each. Four consultants who were hired to work on a special project had the following professional earnings in the previous year: $37,500, $44,000, $46,500, and $61,100.
    What will be the TOTAL DAILY COST to the agency for these four consultants?

    A. $932   B. $824   C. $756   D. $712

18. In a typing and stenographic pool consisting of 30 employees, 2/5 of them are typists, 1/3 of them are senior typists and senior stenographers, and the rest are stenographers. If there are 5 more stenographers than senior stenographers, how many senior stenographers are in the typing and stenographic pool?

    A. 3   B. 5   C. 8   D. 10

19. There are 3330 copies of a three-page report to be collated. One clerk starts collating at 9:00 A.M. and is joined 15 minutes later by two other clerks. It takes 15 minutes for each of these clerks to collate 90 copies of the report.
    At what time should the job be completed if ALL three clerks continue working at the SAME rate without breaks?

    A. 12:00 Noon   B. 12:15 P.M.   C. 1:00 P.M.   D. 1:15 P.M.

20. By the end of last year, membership in the blood credit program in a certain agency had increased from the year before by 500, bringing the total to 2500.
    If the membership increased by the same percentage this year, the TOTAL number of members in the blood credit program for this agency by the end of this year should be

    A. 2625   B. 3000   C. 3125   D. 3250

21. During this year, an agency suggestion program put into practice suggestions from 24 employees, thereby saving the agency 40 times the amount of money it paid in awards. If 1/3 of the employees were awarded $50 each, 1/2 of the employees were awarded $25 each, and the rest were awarded $10 each, how much money did the agency SAVE by using the suggestions?

    A. $18,760   B. $29,600   C. $32,400   D. $46,740

22. Which of the following actions should a supervisor generally find MOST effective as a method of determining whether subordinates need additional training in performing their work?

    A. Compiling a list of absences and latenesses of subordinates
    B. Observing the manner in which his subordinates carry out their various tasks
    C. Reviewing the grievances submitted by subordinates
    D. Reminding his subordinates to consult him if they experience difficulty in completing an assignment

23. Of the following types of letters, the MOST difficult to trace if lost after mailing is the _____ letter.

    A. special delivery
    B. registered
    C. insured
    D. certified

24. Suppose that you are looking over a few incoming letters that have been put in your mail basket. You see that one has a return address on the envelope but not on the letter itself. Of the following, the BEST way to make sure there is a correct record of the return address is to

    A. return the letter to the sender and ask him to fill in his address on his own letter
    B. put the letter back into the envelope and close the opening with a paper clip
    C. copy the address onto a 3"x5" index card and throw away the envelope
    D. copy the address onto the letter and staple the envelope to the letter

25. Although most incoming mail that you receive in an office will pertain to business matters, there are times when a letter may be delivered for your supervisor that is marked *Personal*.
    Of the following, the BEST way for you to handle this type of mail is to

    A. open the letter but do not read it, and route it along with the other mail
    B. read the letter to see if it really is personal
    C. have the letter forwarded unopened to your supervisor's home address
    D. deliver the letter to your supervisor's desk unopened

KEY (CORRECT ANSWERS)

1.	A	11.	C
2.	B	12.	A
3.	A	13.	C
4.	D	14.	C
5.	A	15.	B
6.	D	16.	C
7.	D	17.	D
8.	C	18.	A
9.	A	19.	B
10.	C	20.	C

21.	B
22.	B
23.	D
24.	D
25.	D

EXAMINATION SECTION
TEST 1

DIRECTIONS: Each question or incomplete statement is followed by several suggested answers or completions. Select the one that BEST answers the question or completes the statement. *PRINT THE LETTER OF THE CORRECT ANSWER IN THE SPACE AT THE RIGHT.*

1. A supervisor may be required to help train a newly appointed clerk. Which of the following is LEAST important for a newly appointed clerk to know in order to perform his work efficiently?
    A. Acceptable ways of answering and recording telephone calls
    B. The number of files in the storage files unit
    C. The filing methods used by his unit
    D. Proper techniques for handling visitors

    1.____

2. In your agency you have the responsibility of processing clients who have appointments with agency representatives. On a particularly busy day, a client comes to your desk and insists that she must see the person handling her case although she has no appointment.
   Under the circumstances, your FIRST action should be to
    A. show her the full appointment schedule
    B. give her an appointment for another day
    C. ask her to explain the urgency
    D. tell her to return later in the day

    2.____

3. Which of the following practices is BEST for a supervisor to use when assigning work to his staff?
    A. Give workers with seniority the most difficult jobs
    B. Assign all unimportant work to the slower workers
    C. Permit each employee to pick the job he prefers
    D. Make assignments based on the workers' abilities

    3.____

4. In which of the following instances is a supervisor MOST justified in giving commands to people under his supervision? When
    A. they delay in following instructions which have been given to them clearly
    B. they become relaxed and slow about work, and he wants to speed up their production
    C. he must direct them in an emergency situation
    D. he is instructing them on jobs that are unfamiliar to them

    4.____

5. Which of the following supervisory actions or attitudes is MOST likely to result in getting subordinates to try to do as much work as possible for a supervisor? He
    A. shows that his most important interest is in schedules and production goals
    B. consistently pressures his staff to get the work out

    5.____

25

C. never fails to let them know he is in charge
D. considers their abilities and needs while requiring that production goals be met

6. Assume that a supervisor has been explaining certain regulations to a new clerk under his supervision.
The MOST efficient way for the supervisor to make sure that the clerk has understood the explanation is to
   A. give him written materials on the regulations
   B. ask him if he has any further questions about the regulations
   C. ask him specific questions based on what has just been explained to him
   D. watch the way he handles a situation involving these regulations

6._____

7. One of your unit clerks has been assigned to work for a Mr. Jones in another office for several days. At the end of the first day, Mr. Jones, saying the clerk was not satisfactory, asks that she not be assigned to him again. This clerk is one of your most dependable workers, and no previous complaints about her work have come to you from any other outside assignments.
To get to the root of this situation, your FIRST action should be to
   A. ask Mr. Jones to explain in what way her work was unsatisfactory
   B. ask the clerk what she did that Mr. Jones considered unsatisfactory
   C. check with supervisors for whom she previously worked to see if your own rating of her is in error
   D. tell Mr. Jones to pick the clerk he would prefer to have work for him the next time

7._____

8. A senior typist, still on probation, is instructed to type, as quickly as possible, one section of a draft of a long, complex report. Her part must be typed and readable before another part of the report can be written. Asked when she can have the report ready, she gives her supervisor an estimate of a day longer than she knows it will actually take. She then finishes the job a day sooner than the date given her supervisor.
The judgment shown by the senior typist in giving an overestimate of time in a situation like this is, in general,
   A. *good*, because it prevents the supervisor from thinking she works slowly
   B. *good*, because it keeps unrealistic supervisors from expecting too much
   C. *bad*, because she should have used the time left to further check and proofread her work
   D. *bad*, because schedules and plans for other parts of the project may have been based on her false estimate

8._____

9. Suppose a new clerk, still on probation, is placed under your supervision and refuses to do a job you ask him to do.
What is the FIRST thing you should do?
   A. Explain that you are the supervisor and he must follow your instructions
   B. Tell him he may be suspended if he refuses
   C. Ask someone else to do the job and rate him accordingly
   D. Ask for his reason for objecting to the request

9._____

10. As a supervisor of a small group of people, you have blamed worker A for something that you later find out was really done by worker B.
    The BEST thing for you to do now would be to
    A. say nothing to worker A but criticize worker B for his mistake while worker A is near so that A will realize that you know who made the mistake
    B. speak to each worker separately, apologize to worker A for your mistake, and discuss worker B's mistake with him
    C. bring both workers together, apologize to worker A for your mistake, and discuss worker B's mistake with him
    D. say nothing now but be careful about mixing up worker A with worker B in the future

11. You have just learned one of your staff is grumbling that she thinks you are not pleased with her work. As far as you're concerned, this isn't true at all. In fact, you've paid no particular attention to this worker lately because you've been very busy. You have just finished preparing an important report and *breaking in* a new clerk.
    Under the circumstances, the BEST thing to do is
    A. ignore her; after all, it's just a figment of her imagination
    B. discuss the matter with her now to try to find out and eliminate the cause of this problem
    C. tell her not to worry about it; you haven't had time to think about her work
    D. make a note to meet with her at a later date in order to straighten out the situation

12. A most important job of a supervisor is to positively motivate employees to increase their work production.
    Which of the following LEAST indicates that a group of workers has been positively motivated?
    A. Their work output becomes constant and stable.
    B. Their cooperation at work becomes greater.
    C. They begin to show pride in the product of their work.
    D. They show increased interest in their work

13. Which of the following traits would be LEAST important in considering a person for a merit increase?
    A. Punctuality   B. Using initiative successfully
    C. High rate of production D. Resourcefulness

14. Of the following, the action LEAST likely to gain a supervisor the cooperation of his staff is for him to
    A. give each person consideration as an individual
    B. be as objective as possible when evaluating work performance
    C. rotate the least popular assignments
    D. expect subordinates to be equally competent

15. It has been said that, for the supervisor, nothing can beat the *face-to-face* communication of talking to one subordinate at a time.
    This method is, however, LEAST appropriate to use when
    A. supervisor is explaining a change in general office procedure
    B. subject is of personal importance
    C. supervisor is conducting a yearly performance evaluation of all employees
    D. supervisor must talk to some of his employees concerning their poor attendance and punctuality

16. While you are on the telephone answering a question about your agency, a visitor comes to your desk and starts to ask you a question. There is no emergency or urgency in either situation, that of the phone call or that of answering the visitor's question.
    In this case, you should
    A. continue to answer the person on the telephone until you are finished and then tell the visitor you are sorry to have kept him waiting
    B. excuse yourself to the person on the telephone and tell the visitor that you will be with him as soon as you have finished on the phone
    C. explain to the person on the telephone that you have a visitor and must shorten the conversation
    D. continue to answer the person on the phone while looking up occasionally at the visitor to let him know that you know he is waiting

17. While speaking on the telephone to someone who called, you are disconnected.
    The FIRST thing you should do is
    A. hang up but try to keep your line free to receive the call back
    B. immediately get the dial tone and continually dial the person who called you until you reach him
    C. signal the switchboard operator and ask her to re-establish the connection
    D. dial O for Operator and explain that you were disconnected

18. The type of speech used by an office worker in telephone conversations greatly affects the communicator.
    Of the following, the BEST way to express your ideas when telephoning is with a vocabulary that consists mainly of _____ words.
    A. formal, intellectual sounding B. often used colloquial
    C. technical, emphatic D. simple, descriptive

19. Suppose a clerk under your supervision has taken a personal phone call and is at the same time needed to answer a question regarding an assignment being handled by another member of your office. He appears confused as to what he should do. How should you instruct him later as to how to handle a similar situation?
    You should tell him to
    A. tell the caller to hold on while he answers the question
    B. tell the caller to call back a little later

C. return the call during an assigned break
D. finish the conversation quickly and answer the question

20. You are asked to place a telephone call by your supervisor. When you place the call, you receive what appears to be a wrong number.
Of the following, you should FIRST
A. check the number with your supervisor to see if the number he gave you is correct
B. ask the person on the other end what his number is and who he is
C. check with the person on the other end to see if the number you dialed is the number you received
D. apologize to the person on the other end for disturbing him and hang up

Questions 21-30.

DIRECTIONS: WORD MEANING
Each of Questions 21 through 30 contains a word in capitals followed by four suggested meanings of the word. For each question, choose the BEST meaning and write the letter of the best meaning in the space at the right.

21. ACCURATE
    A. correct   B. useful   C. afraid   D. careless

22. ALTER
    A. copy   B. change   C. repeat   D. agree

23. DOCUMENT
    A. outline   B. agreement   C. blueprint   D. record

24. INDICATE
    A. listen   B. show   C. guess   D. try

25. INVENTORY
    A. custom   B. discovery   C. warning   D. list

26. ISSUE
    A. annoy   B. use up   C. give out   D. gain

27. NOTIFY
    A. inform   B. promise   C. approve   D. strength

28. ROUTINE
    A. path   B. mistake   C. habit   D. journey

29. TERMINATE
    A. rest   B. start   C. deny   D. end

30. TRANSMIT
    A. put in   B. send   C. stop   D. go across

Questions 31-35.

DIRECTIONS: READING COMPREHENSION
Questions 31 through 35 test how well you understand what you read. It will be necessary for you to read carefully because your answers to these questions should be based SOLELY on the information given in the following paragraphs.

    The recipient gains an impression of a typewritten letter before he begins to read the message. Factors which provide for a good first impression include margins and spacing that are visually pleasing, formal parts of the letter which are correctly placed according to the style of the letter, copy which is free of obvious erasures and over-strikes, and transcript that is even and clear. The problem for the typist is that of how to produce that first, positive impression of her work.
    There are several general rules which a typist can follow when she wishes to prepare a properly spaced letter on a sheet of letterhead. Ordinarily, the width of a letter should not be less than four inches nor more than six inches. The side margins should also have a desirable relation to the bottom margin and the space between the letterhead and the body of the letter. Usually the most appealing arrangement is when the side margins are even and the bottom margin is slightly wider than the side margins. In some offices, however, standard line length is used for all business letters, and the secretary then varies the spacing between the date line and the inside address according to the length of the letter.

31. The BEST title for the above paragraphs would be
   A. Writing Office Letters
   B. Making Good First Impressions
   C. Judging Well-Typed Letters
   D. Good Placing and Spacing for Office Letters

32. According to the above paragraphs, which of the following might be considered the way in which people very quickly judge the quality of work which has been typed?
By
   A. measuring the margins to see if they are correct
   B. looking at the spacing and cleanliness of the typescript
   C. scanning the body of the letter for meaning
   D. reading the date line and address for errors

33. What, according to the above paragraphs, would be definitely UNDESIRABLE as the average line length of a typed letter?
   A. 4"   B. 5"   C. 6"   D. 7"

34. According to the above paragraphs, when the line length is kept standard, the secretary
   A. does not have to vary the spacing at all since this also is standard
   B. adjusts the spacing between the date line and inside address for different lengths of letters
   C. uses the longest line as a guideline for spacing between the date line and inside address
   D. varies the number of spaces between the lines

35. According to the above paragraphs, side margins are MOST pleasing when they 35._____
   A. are even and somewhat smaller than the bottom margin
   B. are slightly wider than the bottom margin
   C. vary with the length of the letter
   D. are figured independently from the letterhead and the body of the letter

Questions 36-40.

DIRECTIONS: CODING

Name of Applicant	H A N G S B R U K E
Test Code	c o m p l e x i t y
File Number	0 1 2 3 4 5 6 7 8 9

Assume that each of the above capital letters is the first letter of the name of an applicant, that the small letter directly beneath each capital letter is the test code for the applicant, and that the number directly beneath each code letter is the file number for the applicant.

In each of the following Questions 36 through 40, the test code letters and the file numbers in Columns 2 and 3 should correspond to the capital letters in Column 1. For each question, look at each column carefully and mark your answer as follows:
   If there is an error only in Column 2, mark your answer A.
   If there is an error only in Column 3, mark your answer B.
   If there is an error in both Columns 2 and 3, mark your answer C.
   If both Columns 2 and 3 are correct, mark your answer D.

The following sample question is given to help you understand the procedure.

SAMPLE QUESTION

| Column 1 | Column 2 | Column 3 |
| AKEHN | otyci | 18902 |

In Column 2, the final test code letter *i* should be *m*. Column 3 is correctly coded in Column 1. Since there is an error only in Column 2, the answer is A.

	Column 1	Column 2	Column 3	
36.	NEKKU	mytti	29987	36._____
37.	KRAEB	txlye	86095	37._____
38.	ENAUK	ymoit	92178	38._____
39.	REANA	xeomo	69121	39._____
40.	EKHSE	ytcxy	97049	

Questions 41-50.

DIRECTIONS: ARITHMETICAL REASONING
Solve the following problems.

41. If a secretary answered 28 phone calls and typed the addresses for 112 credit statements in one morning, what is the RATIO of phone calls answered to credit statements typed for that period of time?
    A. 1:4   B. 1:7   C. 2:3   D. 3:5

41.____

42. According to a suggested filing system, no more than 10 folders should be filed behind any one file guide, and from 15 to 25 file guides should be used in each file drawer for easy finding and filing.
    The MAXIMUM number of folders that a five-drawer file cabinet can hold to allow easy finding and filing is
    A. 550   B. 750   C. 1,100   D. 1,250

42.____

43. An employee had a starting salary of $32,902. He received a salary increase at the end of each year, and at the end of the seventh year, his salary was $36,738.
    What was his AVERAGE annual increase in salary over these seven years?
    A. $510   B. $538   C. $548   D. $572

43.____

44. The 55 typists and 28 senior clerks in a certain agency were paid a total of $1,943,200 in salaries for the year.
    If the average annual salary of a typist was $22,400, the average annual salary of a senior clerk was
    A. $25,400   B. $26,600   C. $26,800   D. $27,000

44.____

45. A typist has been given a three-page report to type. She has finished typing the first two pages. The first page has 283 words, and the second page has 366 words.
    If the total report consists of 954 words, how many words will she have to type on the third page of the report?
    A. 202   B. 287   C. 305   D. 313

45.____

46. In one day, Clerk A processed 30% more forms than Clerk B, and Clerk C processed 11/4 as many forms as Clerk A.
    If Clerk B processed 40 forms, how many MORE forms were processed by Clerk C?
    A. 12   B. 13   C. 21   D. 25

46.____

47. A clerk who earns a gross salary of $452 every week has the following deductions taken from her paycheck: 17½% for City, State, Federal taxes, and for Social Security, $1.20 for health insurance, and $6.10 for union dues.
    The amount of her take-home pay is
    A. $286.40   B. $312.40   C. $331.60   D. $365.60

47.____

48. In 2022 an agency spent $400 to buy pencils at a cost of $1 a dozen. If the agency used ¾ of these pencils in 2022 and used the same number of pencils in 2023, how many MORE pencils did it have to buy to have enough pencils for all of 2023?
   A. 1,200   B. 2,400   C. 3,600   D. 4,800

49. A clerk who worked in Agency X earned the following salaries: $30,070 the first year, $30,500 the second year, and $30,960 the third year. Another clerk who worked in Agency Y for three years earned $30,550 a year for two years and $30,724 the third year.
The DIFFERENCE between the average salaries received by both clerks over a three-year period is
   A. $98   B. $102   C. $174   D. $282

50. An employee who works over 40 hours in any week receives overtime payment for the extra hours at time and one-half (1½ times) his hourly rate of pay. An employee who earns $15.60 an hour works a total of 45 hours during a certain week.
His TOTAL pay for that week would be
   A. $624.00   B. $702.00   C. $741.00   D. $824.00

KEY (CORRECT ANSWERS)

1. B	11. B	21. A	31. D	41. A
2. C	12. A	22. B	32. B	42. D
3. D	13. A	23. D	33. D	43. C
4. C	14. D	24. B	34. B	44. A
5. D	15. A	25. D	35. A	45. C
6. C	16. B	26. C	36. B	46. D
7. A	17. A	27. A	37. C	47. D
8. D	18. D	28. C	38. D	48. B
9. D	19. C	29. D	39. A	49. A
10. B	20. C	30. B	40. C	50. C

TEST 2

DIRECTIONS: Each question or incomplete statement is followed by several suggested answers or completions. Select the one that BEST answers the question or completes the statement. *PRINT THE LETTER OF THE CORRECT ANSWER IN THE SPACE AT THE RIGHT.*

1. To tell a newly employed clerk to fill a top drawer of a four-drawer cabinet with heavy folders which will be often used and to keep lower drawers only partly filled is
   A. *good*, because a tall person would have to bend unnecessarily if he had to use a lower drawer
   B. *bad*, because the file cabinet may tip over when the top drawer is opened
   C. *good*, because it is the most easily reachable drawer for the average person
   D. *bad*, because a person bending down at another drawer may accidentally bang his head on the bottom of the drawer when he straightens up

1.____

2. If you have requisitioned a ream of paper in order to duplicate a single page office announcement, how many announcements can be printed from the one package of paper?
   A. 200   B. 500   C. 700   D. 1,000

2.____

3. In the operations of a government agency, a voucher is ORDINARILY used to
   A. refer someone to the agency for a position or assignment
   B. certify that an agency's records of financial transactions are accurate
   C. order payment from agency funds of a stated amount to an individual
   D. enter a statement of official opinion in the records of the agency

3.____

4. Of the following types of cards used in filing systems, the one which is generally MOST helpful in locating records which might be filed under more than one subject is the _____ card.
   A. cut   B. tickler
   C. cross-reference D. visible index

4.____

5. The type of filing system in which one does NOT need to refer to a card index in order to find the folder is called
   A. alphabetic   B. geographic   C. subject   D. locational

5.____

6. Of the following, records management is LEAST concerned with
   A. the development of the best method for retrieving important information
   B. deciding what records should be kept
   C. deciding the number of appointments a client will need
   D. determining the types of folders to be used

6.____

7. If records are continually removed from a set of files without *charging* them to the borrower, the filing system will soon become ineffective.
Of the following terms, the one which is NOT applied to a form used in a charge-out system is a
   A. requisition card
   B. out-folder
   C. record retrieval form
   D. substitution card

7._____

8. A new clerk has been told to put 500 cards in alphabetical order. Another clerk suggests that she divide the cards into four groups such as A to F, G to L, M to R, and S to Z, and then alphabetize these four smaller groups.
The suggested method is
   A. *poor*, because the clerk will have to handle the sheets more than once and will waste time
   B. *good*, because it saves time, is more accurate, and is less tiring
   C. *good*, because she will not have to concentrate on it so much when it is in smaller groups
   D. *bad*, because this method is much more tiring than straight alphabetizing

8._____

9. The term that describes the equipment attached to an office computer is
   A. interface   B. network   C. hardware   D. software

9._____

10. Suppose a clerk has been given pads of pre-printed forms to use when taking phone messages for others in her office. The clerk is then observed using scraps of paper and not the forms for writing her messages.
It should be explained that the BEST reason for using the forms is that
   A. they act as a checklist to make sure that the important information is taken
   B. she is expected to do her work in the same way as others in the office
   C. they make sure that unassigned paper is not wasted on phone messages
   D. learning to use these forms will help train her to use more difficult forms

10._____

11. Of the following, the one which is spelled INCORRECTLY is
   A. alphabetization   B. reccommendation
   C. redaction   D. synergy

11._____

12. Of the following, the MAIN reason a stock clerk keeps a perpetual inventory of supplies in the storeroom is that such an inventory will
   A. eliminate the need for a physical inventory
   B. provide a continuous record of supplies on hand
   C. indicate whether a shipment of supplies is satisfactory
   D. dictate the terms of the purchase order

12._____

13. As a supervisor, you may be required to handle different types of correspondence.
Of the following types of letters, it would be MOST important to promptly seal which kind of letters?

13._____

A. One marked *confidential*
B. Those containing enclosures
C. Any letter to be sent airmail
D. Those in which carbons will be sent along with the original

14. While opening incoming mail, you notice that one letter indicates that an enclosure was to be included but, even after careful inspection,, you are not able to find the information to which this refers.
Of the following, the thing that you should do FIRST is
A. replace the letter in its envelope and return it to the sender
B. file the letter until the sender's office mails the missing information
C. type out a letter to the sender informing them of their error
D. make a notation in the margin of the letter that the enclosure was omitted

15. You have been given a checklist and assigned the responsibility of inspecting certain equipment in the various offices of your agency.
Which of the following is the GREATEST advantage of the checklist?
A. It indicates which equipment is in greatest demand.
B. Each piece of equipment on the checklist will be checked only once.
C. It helps to insure that the equipment listed will not be overlooked.
D. The equipment listed suggests other equipment you should look for.

16. Your supervisor has asked you to locate a telephone number for an attorney named Jones, whose office is located at 311 Broadway and whose name is not already listed in your files.
The BEST method for finding the number would be for you to
A. call the information operator and have her get it for you
B. look in the alphabetical directory (white pages) under the name Jones at 311 Broadway
C. refer to the heading Attorney in the yellow pages for the name Jones at 311 Broadway
D. ask your supervisor who referred her to Mr. Jones, then call that person for the number

17. An example of material that should NOT be sent by first class mail is a
A. carbon copy of a letter   B. postcard
C. business reply card   D. large catalogue

18. Which of the following BEST describes *office work simplification*?
A. An attempt to increase the rate of production by speeding up the movements of employees
B. Eliminating wasteful steps in order to increase efficiency
C. Making jobs as easy as possible for employees so they will not be overworked
D. Eliminating all difficult tasks from an office and leaving only simple ones

19. The duties of a supervisor who is assigned the job of timekeeper may include all of the following EXCEPT
    A. computing and recording regular hours worked each day in accordance with the normal work schedule
    B. approving requests for vacation leave, sick leave, and annual leave
    C. computing and recording overtime hours worked beyond the normal schedule
    D. determining the total regular hours and total extra hours worked during the week

20. Suppose a clerk under your supervision accidentally opens a personal letter while handling office mail.
    Under such circumstances, you should tell the clerk to put the letter back in the envelope and
    A. take the letter to the person to whom it belongs and make sure he understands that the clerk did not read it
    B. try to seal the envelope so it won't appear to have been opened
    C. write on the envelope *Sorry, opened by mistake*, and put his initials on it
    D. write on the envelope *Sorry, opened by mistake*, but not put his initials on it

Questions 21-25.

DIRECTIONS: SPELLING
Each Question 21 through 25 consists of three words. In each question, one of the words may be spelled incorrectly or all three may be spelled correctly. For each question, if one of the words is spelled incorrectly, write the letter of the incorrect word in the space at the right. If all three words are spelled correctly, write the letter D in the space at the right.

SAMPLE I: (A) guide (B) departmint (C) stranger
SAMPLE II: (A) comply (B) valuable (C) window

In Sample Question I, *departmint* is incorrect. It should be spelled *department*. Therefore, B is the answer to Sample Question 1.
In Sample Question II, all three words are spelled correctly. Therefore D is the answer to Sample Question II.

21. A. argument   B. reciept   C. complain
22. A. sufficient B. postpone   C. visible
23. A. expirience B. dissatisfy   C. alternate
24. A. occurred   B. noticable   C. appendix
25. A. anxious   B. guarantee   C. calender

Questions 26-30.

DIRECTIONS: ENGLISH USAGE
Each Question 26 through 30 contains a sentence. Read each sentence carefully to decide whether it is correct. Then, in the space at the right, mark your answer:
A. if the sentence is incorrect because of bad grammar or sentence structure
B. of the sentence is incorrect because of bad punctuation
C. if the sentence is incorrect because of bad capitalization
D. if the sentence is correct

Each incorrect sentence has only one type of error. Consider a sentence correct if it has no errors, although there may be other correct ways of saying the same thing.

SAMPLE QUESTION I: One of our clerks were promoted yesterday.
The subject of this sentence is *one*, so the verb should be *was promoted* instead of *were promoted*. Since the sentence is incorrect because of bad grammar, the answer to Sample Question I is A.

SAMPLE QUESTION II: Between you and me, I would prefer not going there.
Since this sentence is correct, the answer to Sample Question II is D.

26. The National alliance of Businessmen is trying to persuade private businesses to hire youth in the summertime.   26.____

27. The supervisor who is on vacation, is in charge of processing vouchers.   27.____

28. The activity of the committee at its conferences is always stimulating.   28.____

29. After checking the addresses again, the letters went to the mailroom.   29.____

30. The director, as well as the employees, are interested in sharing the dividends.   30.____

Questions 31-40.

DIRECTIONS: FILING
Each Question 31 through 40 contains four names. For each question, choose the name that should be FIRST if the four names are to be arranged in alphabetical order in accordance with the Rules for Alphabetical Filing given below. Read these rules carefully. Then, for each question, indicate in the correspondingly numbered space at the right the letter before the name that should be FIRST in alphabetical order.

RULES FOR ALPHABETICAL FILING

Names of People

1. The names of people are filed in strict alphabetical order, first according to the last name, then according to first name or initial, and finally according to middle name or initial. For example: George Allen comes before Edward Bell, and Leonard P. Reston comes before Lucille B. Reston.

2. When last names are the same, for example A. Green and Agnes Green, the one with the initial comes before the one with the name written out when the first initials are identical.

3. When first and last names are alike and the middle initial is given, for example John David Doe and John Devoe Doe, the names should be filed in the alphabetical order of the middle names.

4. When first and last names are the same, a name without a middle initial comes before one with a middle name or initial. For example, John Doe comes before both John A. Doe and John Alan Doe.

5. When first and last names are the same, a name with a middle initial comes before one with a middle name beginning with the same initial. For example: Jack R. Herts comes before Jack Richard Hertz.

6. Prefixes such as De, O', Mac, Mc, and Van are filed as written and are treated as part of the names to which they are connected. For example: Robert O'Dea is filed before David Olsen.

7. Abbreviated names are treated as if they were spelled out. For example: Chas. is filed as Charles and Thos. is filed as Thomas.

8. Titles and designations such as Dr., Mr., and Prof. are disregarded in filing.

Names of Organizations

1. The names of business organizations are filed according to the order in which each word in the name appears. When an organization name bears the name of a person, it is filed according to the rules for filing names of people as given above. For example, William Smith Service Co. comes before Television Distributors, Inc.

2. Where bureau, board, office or department appears as the first part of the title of a governmental agency, that agency should be filed under the word in the title expressing the chief function of the agency. For example: Bureau of the Budget would be filed as if written Budget, (Bureau of the). The Department of Personnel would be filed as if written Personnel (Department of).

3. When the following words are part of an organization, they are disregarded: the, of, and.

4. When there are numbers in a name, they are treated as if they were spelled out. For example: 10th Street Bootery is filed as Tenth Street Bootery.

SAMPLE QUESTION:
A. Jane Earl (2)
B. James A. Earle (4)
C. James Earl (1)
D. J. Earle (3)

The numbers in parentheses show the proper alphabetical order in which these names should be filed. Since the name that should be filed FIRST is James Earl, the answer to the sample question is C.

31. A. Majorca Leather Goods B. Robert Majorca and Sons 31._____
    C. Maintenance Management Corp. D. Majestic Carpet Mills

32. A. Municipal Telephone Service B. Municipal Reference Library 32._____
    C. Municipal Credit Union D. Municipal Broadcasting System

33. A. Robert B. Pierce B. R. Bruce Pierce 33._____
    C. Ronald Pierce D. Robert Bruce Pierce

34. A. Four Seasons Sports Club B. 14 Street Shopping Center 34._____
    C. Forty Thieves Restaurant D. 42nd St. Theaters

35. A. Franco Franceschini B. Amos Franchini 35._____
    C. Sandra Franceschia D. Lilie Franchinesca

36. A. Chas. A. Levine B. Kurt Levene 36._____
    C. Charles Levine D. Kurt E. Levene

37. A. Prof. Geo. Kinkaid B. Mr. Alan Kinkaid 37._____
    C. Dr. Albert A. Kinkade D. Kincade Liquors Inc.

38. A. Department of Public Events B. Office of the Public Administrator 38._____
    C. Queensborough Public Library D. Department of Public Health

39. A. Martin Luther King, Jr. Towers B. Metro North Plaza 39._____
    C. Manhattanville Houses D. Marble Hill Houses

40. A. Dr. Arthur Davids B. The David Check Cashing Service 40._____
    C. A.C. Davidsen D. Milton Davidoff

Questions 41-45.

DIRECTIONS: READING COMPREHENSION
Questions 41 through 45 test how well you understand what you read. It will be necessary for you to read carefully because your answers to these questions should be based SOLELY on the information given in the following paragraph.

Work standards presuppose an ability to measure work. Measurement in office management is needed for several reasons. First, it is necessary to evaluate the overall efficiency of the office itself. It is then essential to measure the efficiency of each particular section or unit and that of the individual worker. To plan and control the work of sections and units, one must have measurement. A program of measurement goes hand in hand with a program of standards. One can have measurement without standards, but one cannot have work standards without measurement. Providing data on amount of work done and time expended, measurement does not deal with the amount of energy expended by an individual although in many cases such energy may be in direct proportion to work output. Usually from two-thirds to three fourths of all work can be measured. However, less than two-thirds of all work is actually measured because measurement difficulties are encountered when office work is non-repetitive and irregular, or when it is primarily mental rather than manual. These obstacles are often used as excuses for non-measurement far more frequently than is justified.

41. According to the paragraph, an office manager cannot set work standards unless he can
    A. plan the amount of work to be done
    B. control the amount of work that is done
    C. estimate accurately the quantity of work done
    D. delegate the amount of work to be done to efficient workers

42. According to the paragraph, the type of office work that would be MOST difficult to measure would be
    A. checking warrants for accuracy of information
    B. recording payroll changes
    C. processing applications
    D. making up a new system of giving out supplies

43. According to the paragraph, the actual amount of work that is measured is _____ of all work.
    A. less than two-thirds
    B. two-thirds to three-fourths
    C. less than three-sixths
    D. more than three-fourths

44. Which of the following would be MOST difficult to determine by using measurement techniques?
    A. The amount of work that is accomplished during a certain period of time
    B. The amount of work that should be planned for a period of time
    C. How much time is needed to do a certain task
    D. The amount of incentive a person must have to do his job

45. The one of the following which is the MOST suitable title for the paragraph is:
    A. How Measurement of Office Efficiency Depends on Work Standards
    B. Using Measurement for Office Management and Efficiency
    C. Work Standards and the Efficiency of the Office Worker
    D. Managing the Office Using Measured Work Standards

Questions 46-50.

DIRECTIONS: INTERPRETING STATISTICAL DATA
Questions 46 through 50 are to be answered using the information given in the following table.

AGE COMPOSITION IN THE LABOR FORCE IN CITY A
(2010-2020)

	Age Group	2010	2015	2020
Men	14-24	8,430	10,900	14,340
	25-44	22,200	22,350	26,065
	45+	17,550	19,800	21,970
Women	14-24	4,450	6,915	7,680
	25-44	9,080	10,010	11,550
	45+	7,325	9,470	13,180

46. The GREATEST increase in the number of people in the labor force between 2010 and 2015 occurred among
    A. men between the ages of 14 and 24
    B. men age 45 and over
    C. women between the ages of 14 and 24
    D. women age 45 and over

47. If the total number of women of all ages in the labor force increases from 2020 to 2025 by the same number as it did from 2015 to 2020, the TOTAL number of women of all ages in the labor force in 2025 will be
    A. 27,425   B. 29,675   C. 37,525   D. 38,425

48. The total increase in number of women in the labor force from 2010 to 2015 differs from the total increase of men in the same years by being _____ than that of men.
    A. 770 less   B. 670 more   C. 770 more   D. 1,670 more

49. In the year 2010, the proportion of married women in each group was as follows: 1/5 of the women in the 14-24 age group, 1/4 of those in the 25-44 age group, and 2/5 of those 45 and over.
    How many married women were in the labor force in 2010?
    A. 4,625   B. 5,990   C. 6,090   D. 7,910

50. The 14-24 age group of men in the labor force from 2010 to 2020 increased by APPROXIMATELY
    A. 40%   B. 65%   C. 70%   D. 75%

KEY (CORRECT ANSWERS)

1. B	11. B	21. B	31. C	41. C
2. B	12. B	22. D	32. D	42. D
3. C	13. A	23. A	33. B	43. A
4. C	14. D	24. B	34. D	44. D
5. A	15. C	25. C	35. C	45. B
6. C	16. C	26. C	36. B	46. A
7. C	17. D	27. B	37. D	47. D
8. B	18. B	28. D	38. B	48. B
9. C	19. B	29. A	39. A	49. C
10. A	20. C	30. A	40. B	50. C

EXAMINATION SECTION
TEST 1

DIRECTIONS: Each question or incomplete statement is followed by several suggested answers or completions. Select the one that BEST answers the question or completes the statement. *PRINT THE LETTER OF THE CORRECT ANSWER IN THE SPACE AT THE RIGHT.*

Questions 1-10.

WORD MEANING

DIRECTIONS: Each question from 1 to 10 contains a word in capitals followed by four suggested meanings of the word. For each question, choose the best meaning. *PRINT THE LETTER OF THE CORRECT ANSWER IN THE SPACE AT THE RIGHT.*

1. ACCURATE
   A. correct   B. useful   C. afraid   D. careless

2. ALTER
   A. copy   B. change   C. report   D. agree

3. DOCUMENT
   A. outline   B. agreement   C. blueprint   D. record

4. INDICATE
   A. listen   B. show   C. guess   D. try

5. INVENTORY
   A. custom   B. discovery   C. warning   D. list

6. ISSUE
   A. annoy   B. use up   C. give out   D. gain

7. NOTIFY
   A. inform   B. promise   C. approve   D. strengthen

8. ROUTINE
   A. path   B. mistake   C. habit   D. journey

9. TERMINATE
   A. rest   B. start   C. deny   D. end

10. TRANSMIT
    A. put in   B. send   C. stop   D. go across

45

Questions 11-15.

READING COMPREHENSION

DIRECTIONS: Questions 11 through 15 test how well you understand what you read. It will be necessary for you to read carefully because your answers to these questions should be based ONLY on the information given in the following paragraphs.

The recipient gains an impression of a typewritten letter before he begins to read the message. Pastors which provide for a good first impression include margins and spacing that are visually pleasing, formal parts of the letter which are correctly placed according to the style of the letter, copy which is free of obvious erasures and over-strikes, and transcript that is even and clear. The problem for the typist is that of how to produce that first, positive impression of her work.

There are several general rules which a typist can follow when she wishes to prepare a properly spaced letter on a sheet of letter-head. Ordinarily, the width of a letter should not be less than four inches nor more than six inches. The side margins should also have a desirable relation to the bottom margin and the space between the letterhead and the body of the letter. Usually the most appealing arrangement is when the side margins are even and the bottom margin is slightly wider than the side margins. In some offices, however, standard line length is used for all business letters, and the secretary then varies the spacing between the date line and the inside address according to the length of the letter.

11. The BEST title for the above paragraphs would be: 11._____

   A. Writing Office Letters
   B. Making Good First Impressions
   C. Judging Well-Typed Letters
   D. Good Placing and Spacing for Office Letters

12. According to the above paragraphs, which of the following might be considered the way in which people very quickly judge the quality of work which has been typed? By   12._____

   A. measuring the margins to see if they are correct
   B. looking at the spacing and cleanliness of the typescript
   C. scanning the body of the letter for meaning
   D. reading the date line and address for errors

13. What, according to the above paragraphs, would be definitely UNDESIRABLE as the average line length of a typed letter?   13._____

   A. 4"   B. 5"   C. 6"   D. 7"

14. According to the above paragraphs, when the line length is kept standard, the secretary   14._____

   A. does not have to vary the spacing at all since this also is standard
   B. adjusts the spacing between the date line and inside address for different lengths of letters
   C. uses the longest line as a guideline for spacing between the date line and inside address
   D. varies the number of spaces between the lines

15. According to the above paragraphs, side margins are MOST pleasing when they   15._____

   A. are even and somewhat smaller than the bottom margin
   B. are slightly wider than the bottom margin
   C. vary with the length of the letter
   D. are figured independently from the letterhead and the body of the letter

Questions 16-20.

CODING

DIRECTIONS:

Name of Applicant	H A N G S B R U K E
Test Code	c o m p l e x i t y
File Number	0 1 2 3 4 5 6 7 8 9

Assume that each of the above capital letters is the first letter of the name of an Applicant, that the small letter directly beneath each capital letter is the test code for the Applicant, and that the number directly beneath each code letter is the file number for the Applicant.

In each of the following Questions 16 through 20, the test code letters and the file numbers in Columns 2 and 3 should correspond to the capital letters in Column 1. For each question, look at each column carefully and mark your answer as follows:

If there is an error only in Column 2, mark your answer A.
If there is an error only in Column 3, mark your answer B.
If there is an error in both Columns 2 and 3, mark your answer C.
If both Columns 2 and 3 are correct, mark your answer D.

The following sample question is given to help you understand the procedure.

SAMPLE QUESTION

Column 1	Column 2	Column 3
AKEHN	otyci	18902

In Column 2, the final test code letter *i.* should be *m*. Column 3 is correctly coded to Column 1. Since there is an error only in Column 2, the answer is A.

	Column 1	Column 2	Column 3	
16.	NEKKU	mytti	29987	16._____
17.	KRAEB	txyle	86095	17._____
18.	ENAUK	ymoit	92178	18._____
19.	REANA	xeomo	69121	19._____
20.	EKHSE	ytcxy	97049	20._____

Questions 21-30.

ARITHMETICAL REASONING

21. If a secretary answered 28 phone calls and typed the addresses for 112 credit statements in one morning, what is the ratio of phone calls answered to credit statements typed for that period of time?

    A. 1:4 B. 1:7 C. 2:3 D. 3:5

22. According to a suggested filing system, no more than 10 folders should be filed behind any one file guide and from 15 to 25 file guides should be used in each file drawer for easy finding and filing.
    The maximum number of folders that a five-drawer file cabinet can hold to allow easy finding and filing is

    A. 550 B. 750 C. 1,100 D. 1,250

23. An employee had a starting salary of $25,804. He received a salary increase at the end of each year, and at the end of the seventh year his salary was $33,476.
    What was his average annual increase in salary over these seven years?

    A. $1,020 B. $1,076 C. $1,096 D. $1,144

24. The 55 typists and 28 senior clerks in a certain city agency were paid a total of $1,943,200 in salaries last year.
    If the average annual salary of a typist was $22,400 the average annual salary of a senior clerk was

    A. $25,400 B. $26,600 C. $26,800 D. $27,000

25. A typist has been given a three page report to type. She has finished typing the first two pages. The first page has 283 words, and the second page has 366 words.
    If the total report consists of 954 words, how many words will she have to type on the third page of the report?

    A. 202 B. 287 C. 305 D. 313

26. In one day, Clerk A processed 30% more forms than Clerk B, and Clerk C processed li times as many forms as Clerk A. If Clerk B processed 40 forms, how many more forms were processed by Clerk C than Clerk B?

    A. 12 B. 13 C. 21 D. 25

27. A clerk who earns a gross salary of $452 every two weeks has the following deductions taken from her paycheck:
    15% for City, State, Federal taxes; 2 1/2% for Social Security; $1.30 for health insurance; and $6.00 for union dues. The amount of her take-home pay is

    A. $256.20 B. $312.40 C. $331.60 D. $365.60

28. In 2005, a city agency spent $2,000 to buy pencils at a cost of $5.00 a dozen.
    If the agency used 3/4 of these pencils in 2005 and used the same number of pencils in 2006, how many more pencils did it have to buy to have enough pencils for all of 2006?

    A. 1,200 B. 2,400 C. 3,600 D. 4,800

29. A clerk who worked in Agency X earned the following salaries: $20,140 the first year, $21,000 the second year, and $21,920 the third year. Another clerk who worked in Agency Y for three years earned $21,100 a year for two years and $21,448 the third year. The difference between the average salaries received by both clerks over a three-year period is

    A. $196   B. $204   C. $348   D. $564

30. An employee who works over 40 hours in any week receives overtime payment for the extra hours at time and one-half (1 1/2 times) his hourly rate of pay. An employee who earns $13.60 an hour works a total of 45 hours during a certain week.
    His total pay for that week would be

    A. $564.40   B. $612.00   C. $646.00   D. $812.00

Questions 31-35.

RELATED INFORMATION

31. To tell a newly-employed clerk to fill a top drawer of a four-drawer cabinet with heavy folders which will be often used and to keep lower drawers only partly filled is

    A. *good*, because a tall person would have to bend unnecessarily if he had to use a lower drawer
    B. *bad*, because the file cabinet may tip over when the top drawer is opened
    C. *good*, because it is the most easily reachable drawer for the average person
    D. *bad*, because a person bending down at another drawer may accidentally bang his head on the bottom of the drawer when he straightens up

32. If a senior typist or senior clerk has requisitioned a *ream* of paper in order to duplicate a single page office announcement, how many announcements can be printed from the one package of paper?

    A. 200   B. 500   C. 700   D. 1,000

33. Your supervisor has asked you to locate a telephone number for an attorney named Jones, whose office is located at 311 Broadway, and whose name is not already listed in your files.
    The BEST method for finding the number would be for you to

    A. call the information operator and have her get it for you
    B. look in the alphabetical directory (white pages) under the name Jones at 311 Broadway
    C. refer to the heading Attorney in the yellow pages for the name Jones at 311 Broadway
    D. ask your supervisor who referred her to Mr. Jones, then call that person for the number

34. An example of material that should NOT be sent by first class mail is a

    A. email copy of a letter   B. post card
    C. business reply card   D. large catalogue

35. In the operations of a government agency, a voucher is ORDINARILY used to   35._____
    A. refer someone to the agency for a position or assignment
    B. certify that an agency's records of financial trans-actions are accurate
    C. order payment from agency funds of a stated amount to an individual
    D. enter a statement of official opinion in the records of the agency

Questions 36-40.

ENGLISH USAGE

DIRECTIONS: Each question from 36 through 40 contains a sentence. Read each sentence carefully to decide whether it is correct. Then, in the space at the right, mark your answer:

(A) if the sentence is incorrect because of bad grammar or sentence structure

(B) if the sentence is incorrect because of bad punctuation

(C) if the sentence is incorrect because of bad capitalization

(D) if the sentence is correct

Each incorrect sentence has only one type of error. Consider a sentence correct if it has no errors, although there may be other correct ways of saying the same thing.

SAMPLE QUESTION I: One of our clerks were promoted yesterday.

The subject of this sentence is *one,* so the verb should be *was promoted* instead of *were promoted.* Since the sentence is incorrect because of bad grammar, the answer to Sample Question I is (A).

SAMPLE QUESTION II: Between you and me, I would prefer not going there.

Since this sentence is correct, the answer to Sample Question II is (D).

36. The National alliance of Businessmen is trying to persuade private businesses to hire youth in the summertime.   36._____

37. The supervisor who is on vacation, is in charge of processing vouchers.   37._____

38. The activity of the committee at its conferences is always stimulating.   38._____

39. After checking the addresses again, the letters went to the mailroom.   39._____

40. The director, as well as the employees, are interested in sharing the dividends.   40._____

Questions 41-45.

FILING

DIRECTIONS: Each question from 41 through 45 contains four names. For each question, choose the name that should be FIRST if the four names are to be arranged in alphabetical order in accordance with the Rules for Alphabetical Filing given below. Read these rules carefully. Then, for each question, indicate in the space at the right the letter before the name that should be FIRST in alphabetical order.

RULES FOR ALPHABETICAL FILING

Names of People

(1) The names of people are filed in strict alphabetical order, first according to the last name, then according to first name or initial, and finally according to middle name or initial. FOR EXAMPLE: George Allen comes before Edward Bell, and Leonard P. Reston comes before Lucille B. Reston.

(2) When last names are the same, FOR EXAMPLE, A. Green and Agnes Green, the one with the initial comes before the one with the name written out when the first initials are identical.

(3) When first and last names are alike and the middle name is given, FOR EXAMPLE, John David Doe and John Devoe Doe, the names should be filed in the alphabetical order of the middle names.

(4) When first and last names are the same, a name without a middle initial comes before one with a middle name or initial. FOR EXAMPLE, John Doe comes before both John A. Doe and John Alan Doe.

(5) When first and last names are the same, a name with a middle initial comes before one with a middle name beginning with the same initial. FOR EXAMPLE: Jack R. Hertz comes before Jack Richard Hertz.

(6) Prefixes such as De, O', Mac, Mc, and Van are filed as written and are treated as part of the names to which they are connected. FOR EXAMPLE: Robert O'Dea is filed before David Olsen.

(7) Abbreviated names are treated as if they were spelled out. FOR EXAMPLE: Chas. is filed as Charles and Thos. is filed as Thomas.

(8) Titles and designations such as Dr., Mr., and Prof, are disregarded in filing.

Names of Organizations

(1) The names of business organizations are filed according to the order in which each word in the name appears. When an organization name bears the name of a person, it is filed according to the rules for filing names of people as given above. FOR EXAMPLE: William Smith Service Co. comes before Television Distributors, Inc.

(2) Where bureau, board, office, or department appears as the first part of the title of a governmental agency, that agency should be filed under the word in the title expressing the chief function of the agency. FOR EXAMPLE: Bureau of the Budget would be filed as if written Budget, (Bureau of the). The Department of Personnel would be filed as if written Personnel, (Department of).

(3) When the following words are part of an organization, they are disregarded: the, of, and.

(4) When there are numbers in a name, they are treated as if they were spelled out. FOR EXAMPLE: 10th Street Bootery is filed as Tenth Street Bootery.

SAMPLE QUESTION:
- A. Jane Earl (2)
- B. James A. Earle (4)
- C. James Earl (1)
- D. J. Earle (3)

The numbers in parentheses show the proper alphabetical order in which these names should be filed. Since the name that should be filed FIRST is James Earl, the answer to the Sample Question is (C).

41.
- A. Majorca Leather Goods
- B. Robert Maiorca and Sons
- C. Maintenance Management Corp.
- D. Majestic Carpet Mills

42.
- A. Municipal Telephone Service
- B. Municipal Reference Library
- C. Municipal Credit Union
- D. Municipal Broadcasting System

43.
- A. Robert B. Pierce
- B. R. Bruce Pierce
- C. Ronald Pierce
- D. Robert Bruce Pierce

44.
- A. Four Seasons Sports Club
- B. 14th. St. Shopping Center
- C. Forty Thieves Restaurant
- D. 42nd St. Theaters

45.
- A. Franco Franceschini
- B. Amos Franchini
- C. Sandra Franceschia
- D. Lilie Franchinesca

Questions 46-50.

SPELLING

DIRECTIONS: In each question, one of the words is misspelled. Select the letter of the misspelled word. *PRINT THE LETTER OF THE CORRECT ANSWER IN THE SPACE AT THE RIGHT.*

46.
- A. option
- B. extradite
- C. comparitive
- D. jealousy

47.
- A. handicaped
- B. assurance
- C. sympathy
- D. speech

48. A. recommend B. carraige
    C. disapprove D. independent   48.____

49. A. ingenuity B. tenet (opinion)
    C. uncanny D. intrigueing   49.____

50. A. arduous B. hideous
    C. iervant D. companies   50.____

KEY (CORRECT ANSWERS)

1. A	11. D	21. A	31. B	41. C
2. B	12. B	22. D	32. B	42. D
3. D	13. D	23. C	33. C	43. B
4. B	14. B	24. A	34. D	44. D
5. D	15. A	25. C	35. C	45. C
6. C	16. B	26. D	36. C	46. C
7. A	17. C	27. D	37. B	47. A
8. C	18. D	28. B	38. D	48. B
9. D	19. A	29. A	39. A	49. D
10. B	20. C	30. C	40. A	50. C'

EXAMINATION SECTION
TEST 1

DIRECTIONS: Each question or incomplete statement is followed by several suggested answers or completions. Select the one that BEST answers the question or completes the statement. *PRINT THE LETTER OF THE CORRECT ANSWER IN THE SPACE AT THE RIGHT.*

1. Which of the following is the acceptable format for typing the date line? 1._____
   A. 12/2/16
   B. December 2, 2016
   C. December 2nd, 2016
   D. Dec. 2 2016

2. When typing a letter, which of the following is INACCURATE? 2._____
   A. If the letter is to be more than one page long, subsequent sheets should be blank, but should match the letterhead sheet in size, color, weight, and texture.
   B. Long quoted material must be centered and single-spaced internally.
   C. Quotation marks must be used when there is long quoted material.
   D. Double spacing is used above and below tables and long quotations to set them off from the rest of the material.

3. Which of the following is INACCURATE? 3._____
   A. When an addressee's title in an inside address would overrun the center of a page, it's best to carry part of the title over to another line and to indent it by two spaces.
   B. It is permissible to use ordinal numbers in an inside address.
   C. In addresses involving street numbers under three, the number is written out in full.
   D. In the inside address, suite, apartment or room numbers should be placed on the line after the street address.

4. All of the following are common styles of business letters EXCEPT 4._____
   A. simplified
   B. block
   C. direct
   D. executive

5. Please select the two choices below that correctly represent how a continuation sheet heading may be typed. 5._____

   I. Page 2
      Mr. Alan Post
      June 25, 2016

   II. Page 2
       Mr. Alan Post
       6-25-16

   III. Mr. Alan Post   -2-   June 25, 2016

   IV. Mr. Alan Post   -2-   6-25-16

   The CORRECT answer is:

   A. I, II   B. II, III   C. I, III   D. II, IV

6. Which of the following is INCORRECT? It is 6._____
   A. permissible to abbreviate honorifics in the inside address
   B. permissible to abbreviate company or organizational names, departmental designations, or organizational titles in the inside address

C. permissible to use abbreviations in the inside address if they have been used on the printed letterhead and form part of the official company name
D. sometimes permissible to omit the colon after the salutation

7. Which of the following is INCORRECT? 7.____

   A. The subject line of a letter gives the main idea of the message as succinctly as possible.
   B. If a letter contains an enclosure, there should be a notation indicating this.
   C. Important enclosures ought to be listed numerically and described.
   D. An enclosure notation should be typed flush with the right margin.

8. Which of the following is INACCURATE about inside addresses? 8.____

   A. An intraoffice or intracompany mail stop number such as DA 3C 61B is put after the organization or company name with at least two spaces intervening.
   B. Words such as *Avenue* should not be abbreviated.
   C. With the exception of runovers, the inside address should not be more than five full lines.
   D. The inside address includes the recipient's courtesy or honorific title and his or her full name on line one; the recipient's title on the next line; the recipient's official organizational affiliation on the next line; the street address on the penultimate line; and the city, state, and zip code on the last line.

9. Which of the following is an INCORRECT example of how to copy recipients when using copy notation? 9.____

   A. cc: Martin A.Sheen
   B. cc: Ms. Connors
          Ms. Grogan
          Ms. Reynolds
   C. CC: Martin A. Sheen
   D. cc: Mr. Right
          Mr. Wrong
          Mr. Perfect

10. When typing a memo, all of the following are true EXCEPT 10.____

    A. it is permissible to use an abbreviation like 1/1/16
    B. the subject line should be underlined
    C. titles such as *Mr.* or *Dr.* are usually not used on the *To* line
    D. unless the memo is very short, paragraphs should be single-spaced and double spacing should be used to separate the paragraphs from each other

11. When typing a letter, which of the following is INACCURATE? 11.____

    A. Paragraphs in business letters are usually single-spaced, with double spacing separating them from each other.
    B. Margin settings used on subsequent sheets should match those used on the letterhead sheet.
    C. If the message contains an enumerated list, it is best to block and center the listed material by five or six more spaces, right and left.
    D. A quotation of more than three typed lines must be single-spaced and centered on the page.

12. A letter that is to be signed by Hazel Alice Putney, but written by Mary Jane Roberts, and typed by Alice Carol Bell would CORRECTLY bear the following set of initials:

    A. HAP:MJR:acb
    B. HAP:MJR:ab
    C. HAP:mjr:acb
    D. HAP:mjr:ab

13. Which of the following is INCORRECT?

    A. My dear Dr. Jones:
    B. Dear Accounting Department:
    C. Dear Dr. Jones:
    D. Dear Mr. Al Lee, Esq.:

14. Which of the following is INCORRECT?

    A. Bcc stands for blind copy or blind courtesy copy.
    B. When a blind copy is used, the notation bcc appears only on the original.
    C. When a blind copy is used, the notation may appear in the top left corner of the letterhead sheet.
    D. If following a letter style that uses indented paragraphs, the postscript should be indented in exactly the same manner.

15. All of the following are true of the complimentary close EXCEPT

    A. it is typed two lines beneath the last line of the message
    B. when using a minimal punctuation system, you may omit the comma in the complimentary close if you have used a colon in the salutation
    C. where the complimentary close is placed may vary
    D. the first word of the complimentary close is capitalized

16. When typing a letter, which of the following is INACCURATE?

    A. Tables should be centered.
    B. If the letter is to be more than one page long, at least three lines of the message itself should be carried over.
    C. The message begins two lines below the salutation in almost all letter styles.
    D. Triple spacing should be used above and below lists to set them off from the rest of the letter.

17. Which one of the following is INCORRECT?

    A. When used, special mailing instructions should be indicated on both the envelope and the letter itself.
    B. Depending upon the length of the message and the available space, special mailing instructions are usually typed flush left, about four spaces below the date line and about two lines above the first line of the inside address.
    C. Certification, registration, special delivery, and overseas air mail are all considered special mailing instructions.
    D. Special mailing instructions should not be typed in capital letters.

18. Which of the following is INCORRECT?

    A. When a letter is intended to be personal or confidential, these instructions are typewritten in capital letters on the envelope and on the letter itself.

B. When a letter is intended to be personal or confidential, these instructions are typewritten in capital letters on the envelope, but not on the letter.
C. A letter marked PERSONAL is an eyes-only communication for the recipient.
D. A letter marked CONFIDENTIAL means that the recipient and any other authorized person may open and read it.

19. All of the following are true in regard to copy notation EXCEPT

    A. when included in a letter, a copy notation should be typed flush with the left margin, two lines below the signature block or two lines below any preceding notation
    B. copy notation should appear after writer/typist initials and/or enclosure notations, if these are used
    C. the copy recipient's full name and address should be indicated
    D. if more than one individual is to be copied, recipients should be listed in alphabetical order according to full name or initials

20. When addressing envelopes, which of the following is INACCURATE?

    A. When both street address and box number are used, the destination of the letter should be placed on the line just above the city, state, and zip code line.
    B. Special mailing instructions are typed in capital letters below the postage.
    C. Special handling instructions should be typed in capital letters and underlined.
    D. The address should be single-spaced.

21. All of the following should be capitalized EXCEPT the

    A. first word of a direct quotation
    B. first word in the continuation of a split, single-sentence quotation
    C. names of organizations
    D. names of places and geographic districts, regions, divisions, and locales

22. All of the following are true about capitalization EXCEPT

    A. words indicating direction and regions are capitalized
    B. the names of rivers, seas, lakes, mountains, and oceans are capitalized
    C. the names of nationalities, tribes, languages, and races are capitalized
    D. civil, military, corporate, royal and noble, honorary, and religious titles are capitalized when they precede a name

23. All of the following are true about capitalization EXCEPT

    A. key words in the titles of musical, dramatic, artistic, and literary works are capitalized as are the first and last words
    B. the first word of the salutation and of the complimentary close of a letter is capitalized
    C. abbreviations and acronyms are not capitalized
    D. the days of the week, months of the year, holidays, and holy days are capitalized

24. All of the following are true EXCEPT

    A. an apostrophe indicates the omission of letters in contractions
    B. an apostrophe indicates the possessive case of singular and plural nouns

C. an apostrophe should not be used to indicate the omission of figures in dates
D. ellipses are used to indicate the omission of words or sentences within quoted material

25. All of the following are true EXCEPT

    A. brackets may be used to enclose words or passages in quotations to indicate the insertion of material written by someone other than the original writer
    B. brackets may be used to enclose material that is inserted within material already in parentheses
    C. a dash, rather than a colon, should be used to introduce a list
    D. a colon may be used to introduce a long quotation

26. All of the following are true EXCEPT a(n)

    A. comma may be used to set off short quotations and sayings
    B. apostrophe is often used to represent the word *per*
    C. dash may be used to indicate a sudden change or break in continuity
    D. dash may be used to set apart an emphatic or defining phrase

27. All of the following are true EXCEPT

    A. a hyphen may be used as a substitute for the word *to* between figures or words
    B. parentheses are used to enclose material that is not an essential part of the sentence and that, if not included, would not change its meaning
    C. single quotation marks are used to enclose quotations within quotations
    D. semicolons and colons are put inside closing quotation marks

28. All of the following are true EXCEPT

    A. commas and periods should be put inside closing quotation marks
    B. for dramatic effect, a semicolon may be used instead of a comma to signal longer pauses
    C. a semicolon is used to set off city and state in geographic names
    D. italics are used to represent the titles of magazines and newspapers

29. According to standard rules for typing, two spaces are left after a

    A. closing parenthesis   B. comma
    C. number   D. colon

30. All of the following are true EXCEPT

    A. rounding out large numbers is often acceptable
    B. it is best to use numerical figures to express specific hours, measures, dates, page numbers, coordinates, and addresses
    C. when a sentence begins with a number, it is best to use numerical figures rather than to spell the number out
    D. when two or more numbers appear in one sentence, it is best to spell them out consistently or use numerical figures consistently, regardless of the size of the numbers

31. All of the following are true about word division EXCEPT
    A. words should not be divided on a single letter
    B. it is acceptable to carry over two-letter endings
    C. the final word in a paragraph should not be divided
    D. words in headings should not be divided

32. All of the following are true of word division EXCEPT
    A. it is preferable to divide words of three or more syllables after the consonant
    B. it is best to avoid breaking words on more than two consecutive lines
    C. words should be divided according to pronunciation
    D. two-syllable words are divided at the end of the first syllable

33. All of the following are true of word division EXCEPT
    A. words with short prefixes should be divided after the prefix
    B. prefixes and combining forms of more than one syllable should be divided after the first syllable
    C. the following word endings are not divided: -gion, -gious, -sial, -sion, -tial, -tion, -tious, -ceous, -cial, -cient, -cion, -cious, and -geous
    D. words ending in -er should not be divided if the division could only occur on the -er form

34. All of the following are true about word division EXCEPT
    A. words should be divided so that the part of the word left at the end of the line will suggest the word
    B. abbreviations should not be divided
    C. the suffixes -able and -ible are usually divided instead of being carried over intact to the next line
    D. when the addition of -ed, -est, -er, or a similar ending causes the doubling of a final consonant, the added consonant is carried over

35. All of the following are true of word division EXCEPT
    A. words with doubled consonants are usually divided between those consonants
    B. it is permissible to divide contractions
    C. words of one syllable should not be split
    D. it is best to try to avoid divisions that add a hyphen to an already hyphenated word

36. All of the following are true of word division EXCEPT
    A. dividing proper names should be avoided wherever possible
    B. two consonants, preceded and followed by a vowel, are divided after the first consonant
    C. even though two adjoining vowels are sounded separately, it is best not to divide between the two vowels
    D. it is best not to divide the month and day when typing dates, but the year may be carried over to the next line

37. Which of the following four statements are CORRECT? It would be acceptable to divide the word
    I. *organization* after the first *a* in the word
    II. *recommend* after the first *m*
    III. *interface* between the *r* and the *f*
    IV. *development* between the *e* and the *l*

    The CORRECT answer is:

    A. I *only*
    B. II, III
    C. II *only*
    D. I, II, III

38. Which of the following is divided INCORRECTLY?

    A. usu-ally
    B. call-ing
    C. pro-blem
    D. micro-computer

39. Which of the following is divided INCORRECTLY?

    A. imag-inary
    B. commun-ity
    C. manage-able
    D. commun-ion

40. Which of the following is divided INCORRECTLY?

    A. spa-ghetti
    B. retro-spective
    C. proof-reader
    D. fix-ed

41. Which of the following is divided INCORRECTLY?

    A. Mr. Han-rahan
    B. control-lable
    C. pro-jectile
    D. proj-ect

42. Which of the following is divided INCORRECTLY?

    A. prom-ise
    B. han-dling
    C. have-n't
    D. pro-duce

43. Which of the following is divided INCORRECTLY?

    A. ship-ped
    B. audi-ble
    C. hypo-crite
    D. refer-ring

44. Which of the following is divided INCORRECTLY?

    A. particu-lar
    B. spac-ious
    C. chang-ing
    D. capac-ity

45. There is a critical need to develop the ability to control the mind, especailly the ability to stop repeating negative thoughts. Often, when we must swallow our anger, we are left running an enless tape of thoughts. We can't stop thinking about what the person said and what we should have said in response. To combat this tendency, it is helpful to practice witnessing our thoughts. If we can remain detached from them, we won't fuel them, and they will just run out of gas. As we watch them, we also learn a lot about ourselves. The catch here is not to judge them. Judging may lead to selfblaming, blaming others, excuses, rationalizations, and other thoughts that just add fuel. Another technique is is substituting positive thoughts for negative ones.

It is difficult to do this in the "heat of the moment". With practice, however, its possible to train the mind to do what we want it to do and to contain what we want it to contain. A mind is like a garden – we can weed it, or we can let it grow wild.
The above paragraph contains a number of typographical errors.
How many lines in this paragraph contain typographical errors?

   A. 5   B. 6   C. 8   D. 9

KEY (CORRECT ANSWERS)

1. B	11. D	21. B	31. B	41. A
2. C	12. A	22. A	32. A	42. A
3. D	13. D	23. C	33. B	43. A
4. C	14. B	24. C	34. C	44. B
5. C	15. B	25. C	35. B	45. C
6. B	16. D	26. B	36. C	
7. D	17. D	27. D	37. B	
8. B	18. B	28. C	38. C	
9. D	19. C	29. D	39. B	
10. B	20. C	30. C	40. D	

TEST 2

DIRECTIONS: Each sentence may or may not contain problems in capitalization or punctuation. If there is an error, select the number of the underlined part that must be changed to make the sentence correct. If the sentence has no error, select choice E. <u>No sentence contains more than one error.</u>

1. Is the choice for <u>P</u>resident of the company<u>,</u> George Dawson<u>,</u> or Marilyn Kappel<u>?</u>
     A   B   C   D
<u>No error</u>
E

1.____

2. "To tell you the truth <u>,</u> I was really <u>disappointed</u> that our <u>F</u>all percentages did not show
                           A   B   C

more sales growth <u>,</u> " remarked the bookkeeper. <u>No error</u>
                 D   E

2.____

3. Bruce gave his <u>U</u>ncle clear directions to go <u>s</u>outh on Maplewood Drive <u>,</u> turn left at the
                  A   B   C

intersection with Birch Lane, and then proceed for two miles until he reached Columbia

<u>C</u>ounty . <u>No error</u>
D   E

3.____

4. Janet hopes to transfer to a <u>c</u>ollege in the <u>e</u>ast <u>d</u>uring her <u>j</u>unior year. <u>No error</u>
                             A   B C   D   E

4.____

5. The <u>D</u>eclaration <u>o</u>f Independence <u>states</u> that we have the right to the pursuit of
        A   B   C

<u>H</u>appiness , but it doesn't guarantee that we'll ever find it. <u>No error</u>
D   E

5.____

6. We campaigned hard for the <u>mayor</u><u>,</u> but we<u>'</u>re still not sure if he'll win against <u>S</u>enator
                                     A   B   C   D

Frankovich. <u>No error</u>
                   E

6.____

7. Mr. <u>Butler'</u>s <u>F</u>ord was parked right behind <u>our's</u> on Atlantic <u>A</u>venue . <u>No error</u>
         A   B   C   D   E

7.____

8. <u>"</u>I respect your <u>opinion,</u> but I cannot agree with <u>it."</u> commented my <u>g</u>randmother.
   A   B   C   D

<u>No error</u>
E

8.____

2 (#2)

9. My friends, of course, were surprised _ when when I did so well on the Math section 9.____
   .......A...........B........................C..D
   of the test. No error
   .... E

10. Dr. Vogel and Senator Rydell decided _ that the meeting would be held on February 6, 10.____
    ......................A.........................B...C
    in Ithaca, New York. No error
    ......D..................... E

11. "Frank_ do you understand what we're telling you?" asked the doctor. No error 11.____
    .........A..B.................C........................D..............E

12. When I asked my daughter what she knew about politics_ she claimed_she 12.____
    ..............................A..B........................C
    knew nothing. No error
    ....D........E

13. "If you went to my high school, dad, you'd see things differently," snapped Sean. 13.____
    .............................A........A.........B.C........D
    No error
    E

14. In Carlos' third year of high school, he took geometry, psychology, french, and chemis- 14.____
    .......A..............................B......B..C..................D
    try. No error
    ....E

15. "When you enter the building," the guard instructed us, "turn left down the long, wind- 15.____
    .................................A.......................................B..C............................D
    ing corridor." No error
    .... E

16. We hope to spend a weekend in the Catskill Mountains in the spring, and we'd like to 16.____
    ....A..............................B....C..D
    go to Florida in January. No error
    .... E

17. A clerk in the department of Justice asked Carol and me if we were there on business or 17.____
    ....A....................B.................C
    just sight- seeing_ . No error
    ....D..........E

18. Jamie joined a cult, Harry's in a rock band, and Carol-Ann is studying chinese literature
                    A   B   C
    at the University of Southern California. No error
            D   E

19. Parker Flash asked if my band had ever played at the
                       A
    Purple Turnip, a club in Orinoco Hills. No error
       B   C   D   E

20. "The gift of the Magi" is a short story by O'Henry that deals with the sad ironies of life.
       A B C D
    No error
     E

21. Darwin's theory was developed, as a result of his trip to the Galapagos Islands.
       A B   C   D
    No error
     E

22. Is 10 Downing street the address of Sherlock Holmes or the British Prime Minister?
         A   B   C   D
    No error
     E

23. While President Johnson was in Office, his Great Society program passed a great deal
            A   B   C   D
    of important legislation. No error
                                   E

24. If, as the American Industrial Health Council's study says, one out of every five can-
       A   B   C
    cers today is caused by the workplace, it is a tragic indictment of what is happening
                                               D
    there. No error
           E

25. According to the Articles of Confederation, Congress could issue money, but it could
                             A   B   C
    not prevent States from issuing their own money. No error
               D   E

4 (#2)

26. "I'd really like to know whos going to be shoveling the driveway this winter," said
                      A B   C D
    Laverne. No error
              E

27. According to Carl Jung the Swiss psychologist, playing with fantasy is the key to cre-
                    A   B   C   D
    ativity. No error
             E

28. Don't you find it odd that people would prefer jumping A off the Golden Gate bridge to
       A   B
    jumping off other bridges in the area? No error
                                    C   D   E

29. While driving through the South, we saw many of the sites of famous Civil war battles..
                                A   B   C   D
    No error
    E

30. Although I have always valued my Grandmother's china, I prefer her collection
                                          A   B   C
    of South American art. No error
       D   E

KEY (CORRECT ANSWERS)

1.	A	16.	E
2.	C	17.	B
3.	A	18.	C
4.	B	19.	C
5.	D	20.	A
6.	E	21.	C
7.	C	22.	B
8.	E	23.	B
9.	D	24.	D
10.	E	25.	D
11.	A	26.	B
12.	B	27.	A
13.	C	28.	B
14.	D	29.	C
15.	E	30.	A

ENGLISH GRAMMAR AND USAGE
EXAMINATION SECTION
TEST 1

DIRECTIONS: In the passages that follow, certain words and phrases are underlined and numbered. In each question, you will find alternatives for each underlined part. You are to choose the one that BEST expresses the idea, makes the statement appropriate for standard written English, or is worded MOST consistently with the style and tone of the passage as a whole. Choose the alternative you consider BEST and write the letter in the space at the right. If you think the original version is BEST, choose NO CHANGE. Read each passage through once before you begin to answer the questions that accompany it. You cannot determine most answers without reading several sentences beyond the phrase in question. Be sure that you have read far enough ahead each time you choose an alternative.

Questions 1-14.

DIRECTIONS: Questions 1 through 14 are based on the following passage.

Modern filmmaking <u>had began</u> in Paris in 1895 with the work of the Lumiere brothers.
　　　　　　　　　　1

Using their <u>invention, the Cinématographe,</u> the Lumières were able to photograph, print,
　　　　　　　　　　　　2

and project moving pictures onto a screen. Their films showed <u>actual occurrences. A</u> train
　　　　　　　　　　　　　　　　　　　　　　　　　　　　　　　　　　　　3

approaching a station, people a factory, workers demolishing a wall.

These early films had neither plot nor sound. But another Frenchman, Georges <u>Méliès,</u>

soon incorporated plot lines <u>into</u> his films. And with his attempts to draw upon the potential of
　　　　　　　　　　　　　　　4

film to create fantasy <u>worlds</u>. Méliès also <u>was an early pioneer from</u> special film effects. Edwin
　　　　　　　　　　　　　5　　　　　　　　　　　　　　6

Porter, an American filmmaker, took Méliès emphasis on narrative one step further. Believing

<u>that, continuity of shots</u> was of primary importance in filmmaking, Porter connected
　　7

<u>images to present,</u> a sustained action. His GREAT TRAIN ROBBERY of 1903 opened a new
　　8

era in film.

<u>Because</u> film was still considered <u>as</u> low entertainment in early twentieth century America,
　　9　　　　　　　　　　　　　　　　　　10

it was on its way to becoming a respected art form. Beginning in 1908, the American director

D.W. Griffith discovered and explored techniques to make film a more expressive medium.

2 (#1)

With his technical contributions, as well as his attempts to develop the intellectual and moral
                              11
potential of film, Griffith helped build a solid foundation for the industry.

  Thirty years after the Lumière brothers' first show, sound had yet been added to the
  12   13
movies. Finally, in 1927, Hollywood produced its first *talkie*, THE JAZZ SINGER. With sound,

modern film coming of age.
             14

1. A. NO CHANGE   B. begun   1._____
    C. began   D. had some beginnings

2. A. NO CHANGE   B. invention—the Cinématographe   2._____
    C. invention, the Cinématgraphe—   D. invention, the Cinématographe

3. A. NO CHANGE   B. actually occurrences, a   3._____
    C. actually occurrences—a   D. actual occurrences: a

4. A. NO CHANGE   B. about   4._____
    C. with   D. to

5. A. NO CHANGE   B. worlds   5._____
    C. worlds' and   D. worlds and

6. A. NO CHANGE   B. pioneered   6._____
    C. pioneered the beginnings of   D. pioneered the early beginnings of

7. A. NO CHANGE   B. that continuity of shots   7._____
    C. that, continuity of shots,   D. that continuity of shots

8. A. NO CHANGE   B. images to present   8._____
    C. that, continuity of shots   D. that continuity of shots

9. A. NO CHANGE   9._____
    B. (Begin new paragraph) in view of the fact that
    C. (Begin new paragraph) Although
    D. Do NOT begin new paragraph) Since

10. A. NO CHANGE   B. as if it were   10._____
    C. like it was   D. OMIT the underlined portion

11. A. NO CHANGE   B. similar to   11._____
    C. similar with   D. like with

3 (#1)

12. A. NO CHANGE
    B. (Begin new paragraph) Consequently, thirty
    C. (Do NOT begin new paragraph) Therefore, thirty
    D. (Do NOT begin new paragraph) As a consequence, thirty

12._____

13. A. NO CHANGE
    B. (Begin new paragraph) Consequently, thirty
    C. (No NOT begin new paragraph) Therefore, thirty
    D. (Do NOT begin new paragraph As a consequence, thirty

13._____

14. A. NO CHANGE   B. comes
    C. came   D. had came

14._____

Questions 15-22.

DIRECTIONS: Questions 15 through 22 are based on the following passage.

One of the most awesome forces in nature is the tsunami, or tidal wave. A tsunami—the word is Japanese for harbor wave, can generate the destructive power of many atomic bombs.
             15

Tsunamis usually appear in a series of four or five waves about fifteen minutes apart.
    16
They begin deep in the ocean, gather remarkable speed as they travel, and cover great instances. The wave triggered by the explosion of Krakatoa in 1883 circled the world in three days.

Tsunamis being known to sink large ships at sea, they are most dangerous when they
     17
reach land. Close to shore, an oncoming tsunami is forced upward and skyward, perhaps as
                                                  18
high as 100 feet. This combination of height and speed accounts for the tsunami's great power.

That *tsunami* is a Japanese word is no accident, due to the fact that no nation
                                                19
frequently has been so visited by giant waves as Japan. Tsunamis reach that country regularly,
  20   21
and with devastating consequences. One Japanese tsunami flattened several towns in

1896, also killed 27,000 people. The 2011 tsunami caused similar loss of life as well as untold
     22
damage from nuclear radiation.

15. A. NO CHANGE
    B. tsunami, the word is Japanese for harbor wave—
    C. tsunami—the word is Japanese for harbor wave—
    D. tsunami—the word being Japanese for harbor wave,

16. A. NO CHANGE
    B. (Begin new paragraph) Consequently, tsunamis
    C. (Do NOT begin new paragraph) Tsunamis consequently
    D. (Do NOT begin new paragraph) Yet, tsunamis

17. A. NO CHANGE   B. Because tsunamis have been
    C. Although tsunamis have been   D. Tsunamis have been

18. A. NO CHANGE   B. upward to the sky,
    C. upward in the sky   D. upward,

19. A. NO CHANGE
    B. when one takes into consideration the fact that
    C. seeing as how
    D. for

20. A. NO CHANGE   B. (Place after *has*)
    C. (Place after *so*)   D. (Place after *visited*)

21. A. NO CHANGE   B. Moreover, tsunamis
    C. However, tsunamis   D. Because tsunamis

22. A. NO CHANGE   B. 1896 and killed 27,000 people
    C. 1896 and killing 27,000 people   D. 1896, and 27,000 people as well

Questions 23-33.

DIRECTIONS: Questions 23 through 33 are based on the following passage.

I was <u>married one</u> August on a farm in Maine. The <u>ceremony, itself, taking</u> place in an
               23   24
arbor of pine boughs <u>we had built and constructed</u> in the yard next to the house. On the morning
                               25
of the wedding day, we parked the tractors behind the shed, <u>have tied</u> the dogs to an oak tree to
                                                                   26
keep them from chasing the guests, and put the cows out to pasture. <u>Thus</u> we had thought of
                                                                               27
everything, it seemed. we had forgotten how interested a cow can be in what is going on

<u>around them.</u> During the ceremony, my sister <u>(who has taken several years of lessons)</u> was to
   28   29
play a flute solo. We were all listening intently when she <u>had began</u> to play. As the first notes
                                                                                      30
reached us, we were surprised to hear a bass line under the flute's treble melody. Looking

around, the source was quickly discovered. There was Star, my pet Guernsey, her head hanging
                    31
over the pasture fence, mooing along with the delicate strains of Bach.

Star took our laughter as being like a compliment, and we took her contribution that way,
                              32
too. It was a sign of approval—the kind you would find only at a farm wedding.

23. A. NO CHANGE   B. married, one
    C. married on an   D. married, in an

24. A. NO CHANGE   B. ceremony itself taking
    C. ceremony itself took   D. ceremony, itself took

25. A. NO CHANGE
    B. which had been built and constructed
    C. we had built and constructed it
    D. we had built

26. A. NO CHANGE   B. tie
    C. tied   D. tying

27. A. NO CHANGE
    B. (Do NOT begin new paragraph) And
    C. (Begin new paragraph) But
    D. (Begin new paragraph (Moreover,

28. A. NO CHANGE   B. around her
    C. in her own vicinity   D. in their immediate area

29. A. NO CHANGE
    B. (whom has taken many years of lessons)
    C. (who has been trained in music)
    D. OMIT the underlined portion

30. A. NO CHANGE   B. begun
    C. began   D. would begin

31. A. NO CHANGE
    B. the discovery of the source was quick
    C. the discovery of the source was quickly made.
    D. we quickly discovered the source.

32. A. NO CHANGE   A. as
    C. just as   D. as if

33. A. NO CHANGE
    C. But it was
    B. Yet it was
    D. Being

Questions 34-42.

DIRECTIONS: Questions 34 through 42 are based on the following passage,

Riding a bicycle in Great Britain is not the same as riding a bicycle in the United States. Americans bicycling in Britain will find some basic fundamental differences in the rules of the
                                                        34
road and in the attitudes of motorists.

Probably most difficult for the American cyclist is adjusting with British traffic patterns.
  35   36
Knowing that traffic in Britain moves on the left-hand side of the road, bicycling once there is the
   37   38
mirror image of what it is in the United States.

The problem of adjusting to traffic patterns is somewhat lessened, however by the respect
                                                                     39
with which British motorists treat bicyclists. A cyclist in a traffic circle, for example, is given the same right-of-way with the driver of any other vehicle. However, the cyclist is expected to obey
                    40
the rules of the road. This difference in the American and British attitudes toward bicyclists may
                        41
stem from differing attitudes toward the bicycle itself. Whereas Americans frequently view bicycles as toys, but the British treat them primarily as vehicles.
                42

34. A. NO CHANGE
    C. basically fundamental
    B. basic and fundamental
    D. basic

35. A. NO CHANGE
    C. Therefore, probably
    B. Even so, probably
    D. As a result, probably

36. A. NO CHANGE
    C. on
    B. upon
    D. to

37. A. NO CHANGE
    C. Because traffic
    B. Seeing that traffic
    D. Traffic

38. A. NO CHANGE
    C. once one is
    B. once you are
    D. OMIT the underlined portion

39. A. NO CHANGE B. also, C. moreover, D. therefore,

40. A. NO CHANGE B. as C. as if D. as with

41. A. NO CHANGE
    B. difference in the American and British attitudes toward bicyclists
    C. difference, in the American and British attitudes toward bicyclists
    D. difference in the American, and British, attitudes toward bicyclists

42. A. NO CHANGE B. toy; C. toys, D. toys; but

Questions 43-51.

DIRECTIONS: Questions 43 through 51 are based on the following passage.

People have always believed that supernatural powers <u>tend toward some influence on</u> lives for good or for ill. Superstition originated with the idea that individuals <u>could in turn,</u> exert influence <u>at</u> spirits. Certain superstitions are <u>so deeply embedded</u> in our culture that intelligent people sometimes act in accordance with them.

43 44 45 46

One common superstitious act is knocking on wood after boasting of good fortune. People once believed that gods inhabited trees and, therefore, were present in the wood used to build houses. Fearing that speaking of good luck within the gods' hearing might anger <u>them, people</u> knocked on wood to deafen the gods and avoid their displeasure.

47

Another superstitious <u>custom and practice</u> is throwing salt over the left shoulder.

48

<u>Considering</u> salt was once considered sacred, people thought that spilling it brought bad luck. Since right and left represented good and evil, the believers used their right hands, which symbolized good, to throw a pinch of salt over their left shoulders into the eyes of the evil gods.

49

<u>Because of this</u>, people attempted to avert misfortune.

50

Without realizing the origin of superstitions, many people exhibit superstitious behavior.

<u>Others avoid</u> walking under ladders and stepping on cracks in sidewalks, without having any idea why they are doing so.

51

8 (#1)

43. A. NO CHANGE
    C. tend to influence on
    C. can influence
    D. are having some influence on
    43.____

44. A. NO CHANGE.
    C. could, in turn
    B. could, turning
    D. could, in turn,
    44.____

45. A. NO CHANGE
    C. toward
    C. of
    D. on
    45.____

46. A. NO CHANGE
    C. deepest embedded
    B. deepest embedded
    D. embedded deepest
    46.____

47. A. NO CHANGE
    C. them: some people
    B. them; some people
    D. them, they
    47.____

48. A. NO CHANGE
    C traditional custom
    B. Custom
    D. customary habit
    48.____

49. A. NO CHANGE
    C. Because
    B. Although
    D. Keeping in mind that
    49.____

50. A. NO CHANGE
    C. Consequently
    B. As a result of this,
    D. In this way,
    50.____

51. A. NO CHANGE
    C. Avoiding
    B. Often avoiding
    D. They avoid
    51.____

Questions 52-66.

DIRECTIONS: Questions 52 through 65 are based on the following passage.

In the 1920s, the Y.M.C.A. sponsored one of the first programs in order to promote
                                                                      52
more enlightened public opinion on racial matters; the organization started special university

classes in which young people could study race relations. Among the guest speakers invited to
        53
conduct the sessions, one of the most popular was George Washington Carver, the scientist

from Tuskegee Institute.

As a student, Carver himself had been active in the Y.M.C.A. He shared its evangelical
                                                                  54
and educational philosophy. However, in 1923, the Y.M.C.A. arranged Carver's first initial
                                        55   56
speaking tour, the scientist accepted with apprehension. He was to speak at several white

colleges, most of whose students had never seen, let alone heard, an educated black man.

9 (#1)

Although Carver's appearances did sometimes cause occasional controversy, but
                                 57   58
his quiet dedication prevailed, and his humor quickly won over his audiences. Nevertheless, for
                                                                                59
the next decade, Carver toured the Northeast, Midwest, and South under Y.M.C.A.

sponsorship. Speaking at places never before open to blacks. On these tours Carver
            60
befriended thousands of students, many of whom subsequently corresponded with his
                                         61
afterwards. The tours, unfortunately were not without discomfort for Carver. There were
   62   63
the indignities of *Jim Crow* accommodations and racial insults from strangers. As a result,
                                                                                  64
the scientist's enthusiasm never faltered. Avoiding any discussion of the political and social
                                           65
aspects of racial injustice; instead, Carver conducted his whole life as an indirect attack to
                                                                                          66
prejudice. This, as much as his science, is his legacy to humankind.

52. A. NO CHANGE   B. to promote   52.____
    C. for the promoting of what is D. for the promotion of what are

53. A. NO CHANGE   C. from which   53.____
    C. that   D. by which

54. A. NO CHANGE   B. Sharing.   54.____
    C. Having Shared   D. Because He Shared

55. A. NO CHANGE   B. 1923   55.____
    C. 1923, and   D. 1923, when

56. A. NO CHANGE   B. Carvers' first, initial   56.____
    C. Carvers first initial   D. Carver's first

57. A. NO CHANGE   B. sometimes did   57.____
    C. did   D. OMIT the underlined portion

58. A. NO CHANGE   B. controversy and   58.____
    C. controversy   D. controversy, however

59. A. NO CHANGE   B. However, for   59.____
    C. However, from   D. For

60. A. NO CHANGE   B. sponsorship and spoke   60.____
    C. sponsorship; and spoke   D. sponsorship, and speaking

61. A. NO CHANGE B. who
    C. them   D. those

62. A. NO CHANGE
    B. later
    C. sometimes later.
    D. OMIT the underlined portion and end the sentence with a period

63. A. NO CHANGE   B. tours, unfortunately, were
    C. tours unfortunately, were   D. tours, unfortunately, are

64. A. NO CHANGE B. So
    C. But   D. Therefore,

65. A. NO CHANGE   B. He avoided discussing
    C. Having avoided discussing D. Upon avoiding the discussion of

66. A. NO CHANGE B. over
    C. on   D. of

Questions 67-75.

DIRECTIONS: Questions 67 through 75 are based on the following passage.

Shooting rapids is not the only way to experience the thrill of canoeing. An ordinary-looking stream, innocent of rocks and white water, can provide adventure, as long as it has three essential features; a swift current, close banks, and has plenty of twists and turns.
                                                          68   69
A powerful current causes tension, for canoeists know they will have only seconds for
70
executing the maneuvers necessary to prevent crashing into the threes lining the narrow streams banks. Of course, the narrowness, itself, being crucial in creating the tension. On a
        71   72
broad stream, canoeists can pause frequently, catch their breath, and get their bearings.

However to a narrow stream, where every minute you run the risk of being knocked down by a
         73   74
low-hanging tree limb, they be constantly alert. Yet even the fast current and close banks would be manageable if the stream were fairly straight. The expenditure of energy required to paddle furiously, first on one side of the canoe and then on the other, wearies both the nerves as well
                                                                                    75
as the body.

67. A. NO CHANGE
    B. They say that for adventure an
    C. Many finding that an
    D. The old saying that an

68. A. NO CHANGE
    B. features
    C. features,
    D. features; these being

69. A. NO CHANGE
    B. there must be
    C. with
    D. OMIT the underlined portion

70. A. NO CHANGE
    B. Thus, a
    C. Therefore, a
    D. Furthermore, a

71. A. NO CHANGE
    B. stream's banks.
    C. streams bank's
    D. banks of the streams

72. A. NO CHANGE
    B. narrowness, itself is
    C. narrowness itself is
    D. narrowness in itself being

73. A. NO CHANGE
    B. near
    C. on
    D. with

74. A. NO CHANGE
    B. the canoer runs
    C. one runs
    D. they run

75. A. NO CHANGE
    B. the nerves as well as the body
    C. the nerves, also, as well as the body
    D. not only the body but also the nerves as well

KEY (CORRECT ANSWERS)

1.	C	21.	A	41.	A	61.	A
2.	A	22.	B	42.	C	62.	D
3.	D	23.	A	43.	B	63.	B
4.	A	24.	C	44.	C	64.	C
5.	B	25.	D	45.	D	65.	B
6.	B	26.	C	46.	A	66.	C
7.	D	27.	C	47.	A	67.	A
8.	B	28.	B	48.	B	68.	B
9.	C	29.	D	49.	C	69.	D
10.	D	30.	C	50.	D	70.	A
11.	A	31.	D	51.	D	71.	B
12.	A	32.	B	52.	B	72.	C
13.	B	33.	A	53.	A	73.	C
14.	C	34.	D	54.	A	74.	D
15.	C	35.	A	55.	D	75.	B
16.	A	36.	D	56.	D		
17.	C	37.	C	57.	C		
18.	D	38.	D	58.	C		
19.	D	39.	A	59.	D		
20.	C	40.	B	60.	B		

EXAMINATION SECTION
TEST 1

DIRECTIONS: In each of the following questions, only one of the four sentences conforms to standards of correct usage. The other three contain errors in grammar, diction, or punctuation. Select the choice in each question which BEST conforms to standards of correct usage. Consider a choice correct if it contains none of the errors mentioned above, even though there may be other ways of expressing the same thought. *PRINT THE LETTER OF THE CORRECT ANSWER IN THE SPACE AT THE RIGHT.*

1. A. Because he was ill was no excuse for his behavior
   B. In insist that he see a lawyer before he goes to trial.
   C. He said "that he had not intended to go."
   D. He wasn't out of the office only three days.

2. A. He came to the station and pays a porter to carry his bags into the train.
   B. I should have liked to live in medieval times.
   C. My father was born in Linville. A little country town where everybody knows everyone else.
   D. The car, which is parked across the street, is disabled.

3. A. He asked the desk clerk for a clean, quiet, room.
   B. I expected James to be lonesome and that he would want to go home.
   C. I have stopped worrying because I have heard nothing further on the subject.
   D. If the board of directors controls the company, they may take actions which are disapproved by the stockholders.

4. A. Each of the players knew their place.
   B. He whom you saw on the stage is the son of an actor.
   C. Susan is the smartest of the twin sisters.
   D. Who ever thought of him winning both prizes?

5. A. An outstanding trait of early man was their reliance on omens.
   B. Because I had never been there before.
   C. Neither Mr. Jones nor Mr. Smith has completed his work.
   D. While eating my dinner, a dog came to the window.

6. A. A copy of the lease, in addition to the Rules and Regulations, are to be given to each tenant.
   B. The Rules and Regulations and a copy of the lease is being given to each tenant.
   C. A copy of the lease, in addition to the Rules and Regulations, is to be given to each tenant.
   D. A copy of the lease, in addition to the Rules and Regulations, are being given to each tenant.

2 (#1)

7. A. Although we understood that for him music was a passion, we were disturbed 7._____
by the fact that he was addicted to sing along with the soloists.
B. Do you believe that Steven is liable to win a scholarship?
C. Give the picture to whomever is a connoisseur of art.
D. Whom do you believe to be the most efficient worker in the office?

8. A. Each adult who is sure they know all the answers will some day realize 8._____
their mistake.
B. Even the most hardhearted villain would have to feel bad about so horrible
a tragedy.
C. Neither being licensed teachers, both aspirants had to pass rigorous tests
before being appointed.
D. The principal reason why he wanted to be designated was because he had
never before been to a convention.

9. A. Being that the weather was so inclement, the party has been postponed for 9._____
at least a month.
B. He is in New York City only three weeks and he has already seen all the
thrilling sights in Manhattan and in the other four boroughs.
C. If you will look it up in the official directory, which can be consulted in the
library during specified hours, you will discover that the chairman and
director are Mr. T. Henry Long.
D. Working hard at college during the day and at the post office during the
night, he appeared to his family to be indefatigable.

10. A. I would have been happy to oblige you if you only asked me to do it. 10._____
B. The cold weather, as well as the unceasing wind and rain, have made us
decide to spend the winter in Florida.
C. The politician would have been more successful in winning office if he
would have been less dogmatic.
D. These trousers are expensive; however, they will wear well.

11. A. All except him wore formal attire at the reception for the ambassador. 11._____
B. If that chair were to be blown off of the balcony, it might injure someone
below.
C. Not a passenger, who was in the crash, survived the impact.
D. To borrow money off friends is the best way to lose them.

12. A. Approaching Manhattan on the ferry boat from Staten Island, an 12._____
unforgettable sight of the skyscrapers is seen.
B. Did you see the exhibit of modernistic paintings as yet?
C. Gesticulating wildly and ranting in stentorian tones, the speaker was the
sinecure of all eyes.
D. The airplane with crew and passengers was lost somewhere in the Pacific
Ocean.

13. A. If one has consistently had that kind of training, it is certainly too late to change your entire method of swimming long distances.
    B. The captain would have been more impressed if you would have been more conscientious in evacuation drills.
    C. The passengers on the stricken ship were all ready to abandon it at the signal.
    D. The villainous shark lashed at the lifeboat with it's tail, trying to upset the rocking boat in order to partake of it's contents.

14. A. As one whose been certified as a professional engineer, I believe that the decision to build a bridge over that harbor is unsound.
    B. Between you and me, this project ought to be completed long before winter arrives.
    C. He fervently hoped that the men would be back at camp and to find them busy at their usual chores.
    D. Much to his surprise, he discovered that the climate of Korea was like his home town.

15. A. An industrious executive is aided, not impeded, by having a hobby which gives him a fresh point of view on life and its problems.
    B. Frequent absence during the calendar year will surely mitigate against the chances of promotion.
    C. He was unable to go to the committee meeting because he was very ill.
    D. Mr. Brown expressed his disapproval so emphatically that his associates were embarassed

16. A. At our next session, the office manager will have told you something about his duties and responsibilities.
    B. In general, the book is absorbing and original and have no hesitation about recommending it.
    C. The procedures followed by private industry in dealing with lateness and absence are different from ours.
    D. We shall treat confidentially any information about Mr. Doe, to whom we understand you have sent reports to for many years.

17. A. I talked to one official, whom I knew was fully impartial.
    B. Everyone signed the petition but him.
    C. He proved not only to be a good student but also a good athlete.
    D. All are incorrect.

18. A. Every year a large amount of tenants are admitted to housing projects.
    B. Henry Ford owned around a billion dollars in industrial equipment.
    C. He was aggravated by the child's poor behavior.
    D. All are incorrect.

19. A. Before he was committed to the asylum he suffered from the illusion that he was Napoleon.
    B. Besides stocks, there were also bonds in the safe.
    C. We bet the other team easily.
    D. All are incorrect.

19.____

20. A. Bring this report to your supervisory.
    B. He set the chair down near the table.
    C. The capitol of New York is Albany.
    D. All are incorrect.

20.____

21. A. He was chosen to arbitrate the dispute because everyone knew he would be disinterested.
    B. It is advisable to obtain the best council before making an important decision.
    C. Less college students are interested in teaching than ever before.
    D. All are incorrect.

21.____

22. A. She, hearing a signal, the source lamp flashed.
    B. While hearing a signal, the source lamp flashed.
    C. In hearing a signal, the source lamp flashed.
    D. As she heard a signal, the source lamp flashed.

22.____

23. A. Every one of the time records have been initialed in the designated spaces.
    B. All of the time records has been initialed in the designated spaces.
    C. Each one of the time records was initialed in the designated spaces.
    D. The time records all been initialed in the designated spaces.

23.____

24. A. If there is no one else to answer the phone, you will have to answer it.
    B. You will have to answer it yourself if no one else answers the phone.
    C. If no one else is not around to pick up the phone, you will have to do it.
    D. You will have to answer the phone when nobodys here to do it.

24.____

25. A. Dr. Barnes not in his office. What could I do for you?
    B. Dr. Barnes is not in his office. Is there something I can do for you?
    C. Since Dr. Barnes is not in his office, might there be something I may do for you?
    D. Is there any ways I can assist you since Dr. Barnes is not in his office?

25.____

26. A. She do not understand how the new console works.
    B. The way the new console works, she doesn't understand.
    C. She doesn't understand how the new console works.
    D. The new console works, so that she doesn't understand.

26.____

27. A. Certain changes in my family income must be reported as they occur.
    B. When certain changes in family income occur, it must be reported.
    C. Certain family income change must be reported as they occur.
    D. Certain changes in family income must be reported as they have been occurring.

27.____

28. A. Each tenant has to complete the application themselves.
     B. Each of the tenants have to complete the application by himself.
     C. Each of the tenants has to complete the application himself.
     D. Each of the tenants has to complete the application by themselves.

28._____

29. A. Yours is the only building that the construction will effect.
     B. Your's is the only building affected by the construction.
     C. The construction will only effect your building.
     D. Yours is the only building that will be affected by the construction.

29._____

30. A. There is four tests left.
     B. The number of tests left are four.
     C. There are four tests left.
     D. Four of the tests remains.

30._____

31. A. Each of the applicants takes a test.
     B. Each of the applicant take a test.
     C. Each of the applicants take tests.
     D. Each of the applicants have taken tests.

31._____

32. A. The applicant, not the examiners, are ready.
     B. The applicants, not the examiners, is ready.
     C. The applicants, not the examiner, are ready.
     D. The applicant, not the examiner, are ready

32._____

33. A. You will not progress except you practice.
     B. You will not progress without you practicing.
     C. You will not progress unless you practice.
     D. You will not progress provided you do not practice.

33._____

34. A. Neither the director or the employees will be at the office tomorrow.
     B. Neither the director nor the employees will be at the office tomorrow.
     C. Neither the director, or the secretary nor the other employees will be at the office tomorrow.
     D. Neither the director, the secretary or the other employees will be at the office tomorrow.

34._____

35. A. In my absence, he and her will have to finish the assignment.
     B. In my absence he and she will have to finish the assignment.
     C. In my absence she and him, they will have to finish the assignment.
     D. In my absence he and her both will have to finish the assignment.

35._____

KEY (CORRECT ANSWERS)

1.	B	11.	A	21.	A	31.	A
2.	B	12.	D	22.	D	32.	C
3.	C	13.	C	23.	C	33.	C
4.	B	14.	B	24.	A	34.	B
5.	C	15.	A	25.	B	35.	B
6.	C	16.	C	26.	C		
7.	D	17.	B	27.	A		
8.	B	18.	D	28.	C		
9.	D	19.	B	29.	D		
10.	D	20.	B	30.	C		

TEST 2

DIRECTIONS: Each question or incomplete statement is followed by several suggested answers or completions. Select the one that BEST answers the question or completes the statement. *PRINT THE LETTER OF THE CORRECT ANSWER IN THE SPACE AT THE RIGHT.*

Questions 1-4.

DIRECTIONS: Questions 1 through 4 consist of three sentences each. For each question, select the sentence which contains NO error in grammar or usage.

1. A. Be sure that everybody brings his notes to the conference.
   B. He looked like he meant to hit the boy.
   C. Mr. Jones is one of the clients who was chosen to represent the district.
   D. All are incorrect.

   1.____

2. A. He is taller than I.
   B. I'll have nothing to do with these kind of people.
   C. The reason why he will not buy the house is because it is too expensive.
   D. All are incorrect.

   2.____

3. A. Aren't I eligible for this apartment.
   B. Have you seen him anywheres?
   C. He should of come earlier.
   D. All are incorrect.

   3.____

4. A. He graduated college in 1982.
   B. He hadn't but one more line to write.
   C. Who do you think is the author of this report?
   D. All are incorrect.

   4.____

Questions 5-35.

DIRECTIONS: In each of the following questions, only one of the four sentences conforms to standards of correct usage. The other three contain errors in grammar, diction, or punctuation. Select the choice in each question which BEST conforms to standards of correct usage. Consider a choice correct if it contains none of the errors mentioned above, even though there may be other ways of expressing the same thought.

5. A. It is obvious that no one wants to be a kill-joy if they can help it.
   B. It is not always possible, and perhaps it never ispossible, to judge a person's character by just looking at him.
   C. When Yogi Berra of the New York Yankees hit an immortal grandslam home run, everybody in the huge stadium including Pittsburgh fans, rose to his feet.
   D. Every one of us students must pay tuition today.

   5.____

6. A. The physician told the young mother that if the baby is not able to digest its milk, it should be boiled.
    B. There is no doubt whatsoever that he felt deeply hurt because John Smith had betrayed the trust.
    C. Having partaken of a most delicious repast prepared by Tessie Breen, the hostess, the horses were driven home immediately thereafter.
    D. The attorney asked my wife and myself several questions.

    6._____

7. A. Despite all denials, there is no doubt in my mind that
    B. At this time everyone must deprecate the demogogic attack made by one of our Senators on one of our most revered statesmen.
    C. In the first game of a crucial two-game series, Ted Williams, got two singles, both of them driving in a run.
    D. Our visitor brought good news to John and I.

    7._____

8. A. If he would have told me, I should have been glad to help him in his dire financial emergency.
    B. Newspaper men have often asserted that diplomats or so-called official spokesmen sometimes employ equivocation in attempts to deceive.
    C. I think someones coming to collect money for the Red Cross.
    D. In a masterly summation, the young attorney expressed his belief that the facts clearly militate against this opinion.

    8._____

9. A. We have seen most all the exhibits.
    B. Without in the least underestimating your advice, in my opinion the situation has grown immeasurably worse in the past few days.
    C. I wrote to the box office treasurer of the hit show that a pair of orchestra seats would be preferable.
    D. As the grim story of Pearl Harbor was broadcast on that fateful December 7, it was the general opinion that war was inevitable.

    9._____

10. A. Without a moment's hesitation, Casey Stengel said that Larry Berra works harder than any player on the team.
    B. There is ample evidence to indicate that many animals can run faster than any human being.
    C. No one saw the accident but I.
    D. Example of courage is the heroic defense put up by the paratroopers against overwhelming odds.

    10._____

11. A. If you prefer these kind, Mrs. Grey, we shall be more than willing to let you have them reasonably.
    B. If you like these here, Mrs. Grey, we shall be more than willing to let you have them reasonably.
    C. If you like these, Mrs. Grey, we shall be more than willing to let you have them.
    D. Who shall we appoint?

    11._____

12.
- A. The number of errors are greater in speech than in writing.
- B. The doctor rather than the nurse was to blame for his being neglected.
- C. Because the demand for these books have been so great, we reduced the price.
- D. John Galsworthy, the English novelist, could not have survived a serious illness; had it not been for loving care.

12.____

13.
- A. Our activities this year have seldom ever been as interesting as they have been this month.
- B. Our activities this month have been more interesting, or at least as interesting as those of any month this year.
- C. Our activities this month has been more interesting than those of any other month this year.
- D. Neither Jean nor her sister was at home.

13.____

14.
- A. George B. Shaw's view of common morality, as well as his wit sparkling with a dash of perverse humor here and there, have led critics to term him "The Incurable Rebel."
- B. The President's program was not always received with the wholehearted endorsement of his own party, which is why the party faces difficulty in drawing up a platform for the coming election.
- C. The reason why they wanted to travel was because they had never been away from home.
- D. Facing a barrage of cameras, the visiting celebrity found it extremely difficult to express his opinions clearly.

14.____

15.
- A. When we calmed down, we all agreed that our anger had been kind of unnecessary and had not helped the situation.
- B. Without him going into all the details, he made us realize the horror of the accident.
- C. Like one girl, for example, who applied for two positions.
- D. Do not think that you have to be so talented as he is in order to play in the school orchestra.

15.____

16.
- A. He looked very peculiarly to me.
- B. He certainly looked at me peculiar.
- C. Due to the train's being late, we had to wait an hour.
- D. The reason for the poor attendance is that it is raining.

16.____

17.
- A. About one out of four own an automobile.
- B. The collapse of the old Mitchell Bridge was caused by defective construction in the central pier.
- C. Brooks Atkinson was well acquainted with the best literature, thus helping him to become an able critic.
- D. He has to stand still until the relief man comes up, thus giving him no chance to move about and keep warm.

17.____

18. A. He is sensitive to confusion and withdraws from people whom he feels are too noisy.
    B. Do you know whether the data is statistically correct?
    C. Neither the mayor or the aldermen are to blame.
    D. Of those who were graduated from high school, a goodly percentage went to college.

19. A. Acting on orders, the offices were searched by a designated committee.
    B. The answer probably is nothing.
    C. I thought it to be all right to excuse them from class.
    D. I think that he is as successful a singer, if not more successful, than Mary.

20. A. $120,000 is really very little to pay for such a wellbuilt house.
    B. The creatures looked like they had come from outer space.
    C. It was her, he knew!
    D. Nobody but me knows what to do.

21. A. Mrs. Smith looked good in her new suit.
    B. New York may be compared with Chicago.
    C. I will not go to the meeting except you go with me.
    D. I agree with this editorial.

22. A. My opinions are different from his.
    B. There will be less students in class now.
    C. Helen was real glad to find her watch.
    D. It had been pushed off of her dresser.

23. A. Almost everyone, who has been to California, returns with glowing reports.
    B. George Washington, John Adams, and Thomas Jefferson, were our first presidents.
    C. Mr. Walters, whom we met at the bank yesterday, is the man, who gave me my first job.
    D. One should study his lessons as carefully as he can.

24. A. We had such a good time yesterday.
    B. When the bell rang, the boys and girls went in the schoolhouse.
    C. John had the worst headache when he got up this morning.
    D. Today's assignment is somewhat longer than yesterday's.

25. A. Neither the mayor nor the city clerk are willing to talk.
    B. Neither the mayor nor the city clerk is willing to talk.
    C. Neither the mayor or the city clerk are willing to talk.
    D Neither the mayor or the city clerk is willing to talk.

26. A. Being that he is that kind of boy, cooperation cannot be expected.
    B. He interviewed people who he thought had something to say.
    C. Stop whomever enters the building regardless of rank or office held.
    D. Passing through the countryside, the scenery pleased us.

27. A. The childrens' shoes were in their closet. 27.____
    B. The children's shoes were in their closet.
    C. The childs' shoes were in their closet.
    D. The childs' shoes were in his closet.

28. A. An agreement was reached between the defendant, the plaintiff, the 28.____
       plaintiff's attorney and the insurance company as to the amount of the
       settlement.
    B. Everybody was asked to give their versions of the accident.
    C. The consensus of opinion was that the evidence was inconclusive.
    D. The witness stated that if he was rich, he wouldn't have had to loan the
       money.

29. A. Before beginning the investigation, all the materials related to the case were 29.____
       carefully assembled.
    B. The reason for his inability to keep the appointment is because of his injury
       in the accident.
    C. This here evidence tends to support the claim of the defendant.
    D. We interviewed all the witnesses who, according to the driver, were still in
       town.

30. A. Each claimant was allowed the full amount of their medical expenses. 30.____
    B. Either of the three witnesses is available.
    C. Every one of the witnesses was asked to tell his story.
    D. Neither of the witnesses are right.

31. A. The commissioner, as well as his deputy and various bureau heads, were 31.____
       present.
    B. A new organization of employers and employees have been formed.
    C. One or the other of these men have been selected.
    D. The number of pages in the book is enough to discourage a reader.

32. A. Between you and me, I think he is the better man. 32.____
    B. He was believed to be me.
    C. Is it us that you wish to see?
    D. The winners are him and her.

33. A. Beside the statement to the police, the witness spoke to no one. 33.____
    B. He made no statement other than to the police and I.
    C. He made no statement to any one else, aside from the police.
    D. The witness spoke to no one but me.

34. A. The claimant has no one to blame but himself. 34.____
    B. The boss sent us, he and I, to deliver the packages.
    C. The lights come from mine and not his car.
    D. There was room on the stairs for him and myself.

35. A. Admission to this clinic is limited to patients' inability to pay for medical care.
    B. Patients who can pay little or nothing for medical care are treated in this clinic.
    C. The patient's ability to pay for medical care is the determining factor in his admission to this clinic.
    D. This clinic is for the patient's that cannot afford to pay or that can pay a little for medical care.

35.____

KEY (CORRECT ANSWERS)

1.	A	11.	C	21.	A	31.	D
2.	A	12.	B	22.	A	32.	A
3.	D	13.	D	23.	D	33.	D
4.	C	14.	D	24.	D	34.	A
5.	D	15.	D	25.	B	35.	B
6.	D	16.	D	26.	B		
7.	B	17.	B	27.	B		
8.	B	18.	D	28.	C		
9.	D	19.	B	29.	D		
10.	B	20.	D	30.	C		

SPELLING
EXAMINATION SECTION
TEST 1

DIRECTIONS: Each question or incomplete statement is followed by several suggested answers or completions. Select the one that BEST answers the question or completes the statement. *PRINT THE LETTER OF THE CORRECT ANSWER IN THE SPACE AT THE RIGHT.*

Questions 1-5.

DIRECTIONS: Questions 1 through 5 consist of four words. Indicate the letter of the word that is CORRECTLY spelled.

1. A. harassment B. harrasment C. harasment D. harrassment   1.____

2. A. maintainance B. maintenence C. maintainence D. maintenance   2.____

3. A. comparable B. comprable C. comparible D. commparable   3.____

4. A. suficient B. sufficiant C. sufficient D. suficiant   4.____

5. A. fairly B. fairley C. farely D. fairlie   5.____

Questions 6-10.

DIRECTIONS: Questions 6 through 10 consist of four words. Indicate the letter of the word that is INCORRECTLY spelled.

6. A. pallor B. ballid C. ballet D. pallid   6.____

7. A. urbane B. surburbane C. interurban D. urban   7.____

8. A. facial B. physical C. fiscle D. muscle   8.____

9. A. interceed B. benefited C. analogous D. altogether   9.____

10. A. seizure B. irrelevant C. inordinate D. dissapproved   10.____

93

KEY (CORRECT ANSWERS)

1. A 6. B
2. D 7. B
3. A 8. C
4. C 9. A
5. A 10. D

TEST 2

DIRECTIONS: Each of Questions 1 through 15 consists of two words preceded by the letters A and B. In each question, one of the words may be spelled INCORRECTLY or both words may be spelled CORRECTLY. If one of the words in a question is spelled INCORRECTLY, print in the space at the right the capital letter preceding the INCORRECTLY spelled word. If both words are spelled CORRECTLY, print the letter C.

1. A. easely   B. readily   1._____
2. A. pursue   B. decend   2._____
3. A. measure   B. laboratory   3._____
4. A. exausted   B. traffic   4._____
5. A. discussion   B. unpleasant   5._____
6. A. campaign   B. murmer   6._____
7. A. guarantee   B. sanatary   7._____
8. A. communication   B. safty   8._____
9. A. numerus   B. celebration   9._____
10. A. nourish   B. begining   10._____
11. A. courious   B. witness   11._____
12. A. undoubtedly   B. thoroughly   12._____
13. A. accessible   B. artifical   13._____
14. A. feild   B. arranged   14._____
15. A. admittence   B. hastily   15._____

KEY (CORRECT ANSWERS)

1. A	6. B	11. A
2. B	7. B	12. C
3. C	8. B	13. B
4. A	9. A	14. A
5. C	10. B	15. A

TEST 3

DIRECTIONS: In each of the following sentences, one word is misspelled. Following each sentence is a list of four words taken from the sentence. Indicate the letter of the word which is MISSPELLED in the sentence. *PRINT THE LETTER OF THE CORRECT ANSWER IN THE SPACE AT THE RIGHT.*

1. The placing of any inflammable substance in any building, or the placing of any device or contrivance capable of producing fire, for the purpose of causing a fire is an attempt to burn.
    A. inflammable
    B. substance
    C. device
    D. contrivence

    1.____

2. The word *break* also means obtaining an entrance into a building by any artifice used for that purpose, or by collussion with any person therein.
    A. obtaining
    B. entrance
    C. artifice
    D. colussion

    2.____

3. Any person who with intent to provoke a breech of the peace causes a disturbance or is offensive to others may be deemed to have committed disorderly conduct.
    A. breech
    B. disturbance
    C. offensive
    D. committed

    3.____

4. When the offender inflicts a grevious harm upon the person from whose possession, or in whose presence, property is taken, he is guilty of robbery.
    A. offender
    B. grevious
    C. possession
    D. presence

    4.____

5. A person who wilfuly encourages or advises another person in attempting to take the latter's life is guilty of a felony.
    A. wilfuly
    B. encourages
    C. advises
    D. attempting

    5.____

6. He maliciously demurred to an ajornment of the proceedings.
    A. maliciously
    B. demurred
    C. ajornment
    D. proceedings

    6.____

7. His innocence at that time is irrelevant in view of his more recent villianous demeanor.
    A. innocence
    B. irrelevant
    C. villianous
    D. demeanor

    7.____

8. The mischievous boys aggrevated the annoyance of their neighbor.
    A. mischievous
    B. aggrevated
    C. annoyance
    D. neighbor

    8.____

9. While his perseverence was commendable, his judgment was debatable.   9._____
    A. perseverence   B. commendable
    C. judgment   D. debatable

10. He was hoping the appeal would facilitate his aquittal.   10._____
    A. hoping   B. appeal
    C. facilitate   D. aquittal

11. It would be preferable for them to persue separate courses.   11._____
    A. preferable   B. persue
    C. separate   D. courses

12. The litigant was complimented on his persistance and achievement.   12._____
    A. litigant   B. complimented
    C. persistance   D. achievement

13. Ocassionally there are discrepancies in the descriptions of miscellaneous   13._____
    items.
    A. ocassionally   B. discrepancies
    C. descriptions   D. miscellaneous

14. The councilmanic seargent-at-arms enforced the prohibition.   14._____
    A. councilmanic   B. seargeant-at-arms
    C. enforced   D. prohibition

15. The teacher had an ingenious device for maintaining attendance.   15._____
    A. ingenious   B. device
    C. maintaning   D. attendance

16. A worrysome situation has developed as a result of the assessment that   16._____
    absenteeism is increasing despite our conscientious efforts.
    A. worrysome   B. assessment
    C. absenteeism   D. conscientious

17. I concurred with the credit manager that it was practicable to charge   17._____
    purchases on a biennial basis, and the company agreed to adhear to this
    policy.
    A. concurred   B. practicable
    C. biennial   D. adhear

18. The pastor was chagrined and embarassed by the irreverent conduct of one   18._____
    of his parishioners.
    A. chagrined   B. embarassed
    C. irreverent   D. parishioners

19. His inate seriousness was belied by his flippant demeanor.   19._____
    A. inate   B. belied
    C. flippant   D. demeanor

20. It was exceedingly regrettable that the excessive number of challenges in the court delayed the start of the trial.
    A. exceedingly
    B. regrettable
    C. excessive
    D. challanges

20.____

KEY (CORRECT ANSWERS)

1.	D	11.	B
2.	D	12.	C
3.	A	13.	A
4.	B	14.	B
5.	A	15.	C
6.	C	16.	A
7.	C	17.	D
8.	B	18.	B
9.	A	19.	A
10.	D	20.	D

TEST 4

Questions 1-11.

DIRECTIONS: Each question consists of three words in each question, one of the words may be spelled incorrectly or all three may be spelled correctly. For each question if one of the words is spelled INCORRECTLY, write the letter of the incorrect word in the space at the right. If all three words are spelled CORRECTLY, write the letter D in the space at the right.

SAMPLE I: (A) guide   (B) departmint   (C) stranger
SAMPLE II: (A) comply   (B) valuable   (C) window

In Sample I, departmint is incorrect. It should be spelled department. Therefore, B is the answer.
In Sample II, all three words are spelled correctly. Therefore, D is the answer.

1. A. argument   B. reciept   C. complain   1.____
2. A. sufficient   B. postpone   C. visible   2.____
3. A. expirience   B. dissatisly   C. alternate   3.____
4. A. occurred   B. noticable   C. appendix   4.____
5. A. anxious   B. guarantee   C. calendar   5.____
6. A. sincerely   B. affectionately   C. truly   6.____
7. A. excellant   B. verify   C. important   7.____
8. A. error   B. quality   C. enviroment   8.____
9. A. exercise   B. advance   C. pressure   9.____
10. A. citizen   B. expence   C. memory   10.____
11. A. flexable   B. focus   C. forward   11.____

Questions 12-15.

DIRECTIONS: Each of Questions 12 through 15 consists of a group of four words. Examine each group carefully; then in the space at the right, indicate
   A.   if only one word in the group is spelled correctly
   B.   if two words in the group are spelled correctly
   C.   if three words in the group are spelled correctly
   D.   if all four words in the group are spelled correctly

12. Wendsday, particular, similar, hunderd   12.____

2 (#4)

13. realize, judgment, opportunities, consistent   13.____

14. equel, principle, assistense, committee   14.____

15. simultaneous, privilege, advise, ocassionaly   15.____

KEY (CORRECT ANSWERS)

1.	B	6.	D	11.	A
2.	D	7.	A	12.	B
3.	A	8.	C	13.	D
4.	B	9.	D	14.	A
5.	C	10.	B	15.	C

TEST 5

DIRECTIONS: Each of Questions 1 through 15 consists of two words preceded by the letters A and B. In each item, one of the words may be spelled INCORRECTLY or both words may be spelled CORRECTLY. If one of the words in a question is spelled INCORRECTLY, print in the space at the right the letter preceding the INCORRECTLY spelled word. If bot words are spelled CORRECTLY, print the letter C.

1. A. justified   B. offering   1._____
2. A. predjudice   B. license   2._____
3. A. label   B. pamphlet   3._____
4. A. bulletin   B. physical   4._____
5. A. assure   B. exceed   5._____
6. A. advantagous   B. evident   6._____
7. A. benefit   B. occured   7._____
8. A. acquire   B. graditude   8._____
9. A. amenable   B. boundry   9._____
10. A. deceive   B. voluntary   10._____
11. A. imunity   B. conciliate   11._____
12. A. acknoledge   B. presume   12._____
13. A. substitute   B. prespiration   13._____
14. A. reputable   B. announce   14._____
15. A. luncheon   B. wretched   15._____

KEY (CORRECT ANSWERS)

1. C   6. A   11. A
2. A   7. B   12. A
3. C   8. B   13. B
4. C   9. B   14. A
5. C   10. C   15. C

TEST 6

DIRECTIONS: Questions 1 through 15 contain lists of words, one of which is misspelled. Indicate the MISSPELLED word in each group. *PRINT THE LETTER OF THE CORRECT ANSWER IN THE SPACE AT THE RIGHT.*

1. A. felony B. lacerate C. cancellation D. seperate 1.____

2. A. batallion B. beneficial C. miscellaneous D. secretary 2.____

3. A. camouflage B. changeable C. embarrass D. inoculate 3.____

4. A. beneficial B. disasterous C. incredible D. miniature 4.____

5. A. auxilliary B. hypocrisy C. phlegm D. vengeance 5.____

6. A. aisle B. cemetary C. courtesy D. extraordinary 6.____

7. A. crystallize B. innoculate C. eminent D. symmetrical 7.____

8. A. judgment B. maintainance C. bouillon D. eery 8.____

9. A. isosceles B. ukulele C. mayonaise D. iridescent 9.____

10. A. remembrance B. occurence C. correspondence D. countenance 10.____

11. A. corpuscles B. mischievous C. batchelor D. bulletin 11.____

12. A. terrace B. banister C. concrete D. masonery 12.____

13. A. balluster B. gutter C. latch D. bridging 13.____

14. A. personnell B. navel C. therefor D. emigrant 14.____

15. A. committee B. submiting 15._____
     C. amendment D. electorate

KEY (CORRECT ANSWERS)

1.	D	6.	B	11.	C
2.	A	7.	B	12.	D
3.	C	8.	B	13.	A
4.	B	9.	C	14.	A
5.	A	10.	B	15.	B

TEST 7

Questions 1-5.

DIRECTIONS: Questions 1 through 5 consist of groups of four words. Select answer
A if only one word is spelled correctly in a group
B if TWO words are spelled correctly in a group
C if THREE words are spelled correctly in a group
D if all FOUR words are spelled correctly in a group.

1. counterfeit, embarass, panicky, supercede   1.____
2. benefited, personnel, questionnaire, unparalelled 2.____
3. bankruptcy, describable, proceed, vacuum   3.____
4. handicapped, mispell, offerred, pilgrimmage   4.____
5. corduroy, interfere, privilege, separator   5.____

Questions 6-10.

DIRECTIONS: Questions 6 through 10 consist of four pairs of words each. Some of the words are spelled correctly; others are spelled incorrectly. For each question, indicate in the space at the right the letter preceding that pair of words in which BOTH words are spelled CORRECTLY.

6. A. hygienic, inviegle   B. omniscience, pittance   6.____
   C. plagarize, nullify   D. seargent, perilous

7. A. auxilary, existence   B. pronounciation, accordance 7.____
   C. ignominy, indegence   D. suable, baccalaureate

8. A. discreet, inaudible   B. hypocrisy, currupt   8.____
   C. liquidate, maintainance   D. transparancy, onerous

9. A. facility; stimulent   B. frugel, sanitary   9.____
   C. monetary, prefatory   D. punctileous, credentials

10. A. bankruptsy, perceptible B. disuade, resilient   10.____
    C. exhilerate, expectancy   D. panegyric, disparate

Questions 11-15.

DIRECTIONS: Each question or incomplete statement is followed by several suggested answers or completions. Select the one that BEST answers the question or completes the statement. PRINT THE LETTER OF THE CORRECT ANSWER IN THE SPACE AT THE RIGHT.

11. The silent *e* must be retained when the suffix *–able* is added to the word
 A. argue B. love C. move D. notice

12. The CORRECTLY spelled word in the choices below is
 A. kindergarden B. zylophone
 C. hemorrhage D. mayonaise

13. Of the following words, the one spelled CORRECTLY is
 A. begger B. cemetary
 C. embarassed D. coyote

14.
 A. dandilion B. wiry C. sieze D. rythmic

15. A. beligerent B. anihilation
 C. facetious D. adversery

KEY (CORRECT ANSWERS)

1.	B	6.	B	11.	D
2.	C	7.	D	12.	C
3.	D	8.	A	13.	D
4.	A	9.	C	14.	B
5.	D	10.	D	15.	C

TEST 8

DIRECTIONS: In each of the following sentences, one word is misspelled. Following each sentence is a list of four words taken from the sentence. Indicate the letter of the word which is MISSPELLED. *PRINT THE LETTER OF THE CORRECT ANSWER IN THE SPACE AT THE RIGHT.*

1. If the administrator attempts to withold information, there is a good likelihood that there will be serious repercussions.
    A. administrator
    B. withold
    C. likelihood
    D. repercussions

2. He condescended to apologize, but we felt that a beligerent person should not occupy an influential position.
    A. condescended
    B. apologize
    C. beligerent
    D. influential

3. Despite the sporadic delinquent payments of his indebtedness, Mr. Johnson has been an exemplery customer.
    A. sporadic
    B. delinquent
    C. indebtedness
    D. exemplery

4. He was appreciative of the support he consistantly acquired, but he felt that he had waited an inordinate length of time for it.
    A. appreciative
    B. consistantly
    C. acquired
    D. inordinate

5. Undeniably they benefited from the establishment of a receivership, but the question of statutary limitations remained unresolved.
    A. undeniably
    B. benefited
    C. receivership
    D. statutary

6. Mr. Smith profered his hand as an indication that he considered it a viable contract, but Mr. Nelson alluded to the fact that his colleagues had not been consulted.
    A. profered
    B. viable
    C. alluded
    D. colleagues

7. The treatments were beneficial according to the optomotrists, and the consensus was that minimal improvement could be expected.
    A. beneficial
    B. optomotrists
    C. consensus
    D. minimal

8. Her frivolous manner was unbecoming because the air of solemnity at the cemetery was pervasive.
    A. frivalous
    B. solemnity
    C. cemetery
    D. pervasive

9. The clandestine meetings were designed to make the two adversaries more amicable, but they served only to intensify their emnity.
   A. clandestine
   B. adversaries
   C. amicable
   D. emnity

10. Do you think that his innovative ideas and financial acumen will help stabalize the fluctuations of the stock market?
    A. innovative
    B. acumen
    C. stabalize
    D. fluctuations

11. In order to keep a perpetual inventory, you will have to keep an uninterrupted surveillance of all the miscellanious stock.
    A. perpetual
    B. uninterrupted
    C. surveillance
    D. miscellanious

12. She used the art of pursuasion on the children because she found that caustic remarks had no perceptible effect on their behavior.
    A. pursuasion
    B. caustic
    C. perceptible
    D. effect

13. His sacreligious outbursts offended his constituents, and he was summarily removed from office by the City Council.
    A. sacreligious
    B. constituents
    C. summarily
    D. Council

14. They exhorted the contestants to greater efforts, but the exhorbitant costs in terms of energy expended resulted in a feeling of lethargy.
    A. exhorted
    B. contestants
    C. exhorbitant
    D. lethargy

15. Since he was knowledgable about illicit drugs, he was served with a subpoena to appear for the prosecution.
    A. knowledgable
    B. illicit
    C. subpoena
    D. prosecution

16. In spite of his lucid statements, they denigrated his report and decided it should be succintly paraphrased.
    A. lucid
    B. denigrated
    C. succintly
    D. paraphrased

17. The discussion was not germane to the contraversy, but the indicted man's insistence on further talk was allowed.
    A. germane
    B. contraversy
    C. indicted
    D. insistence

18. The legislators were enervated by the distances they had traveled during the election year to fullfil their speaking engagements.
    A. legislators
    B. enervated
    C. traveled
    D. fullfil

19. The plaintiffs' attornies charge the defendant in the case with felonious assault. 19.____
    A. plaintiffs' B. attornies
    C. defendant   D. felonious

20. It is symptomatic of the times that we try to placate all, but a proposal for new forms of disciplinery action was promulgated by the staff. 20.____
    A. symptomatic B. placate
    C. disciplinery D. promulgated

KEY (CORRECT ANSWERS)

1.	B	11.	D
2.	C	12.	A
3.	D	13.	A
4.	B	14.	C
5.	D	15.	A
6.	A	16.	C
7.	B	17.	B
8.	A	18.	D
9.	D	19.	B
10.	C	20.	C

TEST 9

DIRECTIONS: Each of Questions 1 through 15 consists of a single word which is spelled either correctly or incorrectly. If the word is spelled CORRECTLY, you are to print the letter C (Correct) in the space at the right. If the word is spelled INCORRECTL, you are to print the letter W (Wrong).

1. pospone 1._____
2. diffrent 2._____
3. height 3._____
4. carefully 4._____
5. ability 5._____
6. temper 6._____
7. deslike 7._____
8. seldem 8._____
9. alcohol 9._____
10. expense 10._____
11. vegatable 11._____
12. dispensary 12._____
13. specemin 13._____
14. allowance 14._____
15. exersise 15._____

KEY (CORRECT ANSWERS)

1.	W	6.	C	11.	W
2.	W	7.	W	12.	C
3.	C	8.	W	13.	W
4.	C	9.	C	14.	C
5.	C	10.	C	15.	W

TEST 10

DIRECTIONS: Each of Questions 1 through 10 consists of four words, one of which may be spelled incorrectly or all four words may be spelled correctly. If one of the words in a question is spelled incorrectly, print in the space at the right the capital letter preceding the word which is spelled INCORRECTLY. If all four words are spelled CORRECTLY, print the letter E.

1. A. dismissal B. collateral 1.____
   C. leisure D. proffession

2. A. subsidary B. outrageous 2.____
   C. liaison D. assessed

3. A. already B. changeable 3.____
   C. mischevous D. cylinder

4. A. supersede B. deceit 4.____
   C. dissension D. imminent

5. A. arguing B. contagious 5.____
   C. comparitive D. accessible

6. A. indelible B. existance 6.____
   C. presumptuous D. mileage

7. A. extention B. aggregate 7.____
   C. sustenance D. gratuitous

8. A. interrogate B. exaggeration 8.____
   C. vacillate D. moreover

9. A. parallel B. derogatory 9.____
   C. admissible D. appellate

10. A. safety B. cumalative 10.____
    C. disappear D. usable

KEY (CORRECT ANSWERS)

1. D   6. B
2. A   7. A
3. C   8. E
4. E   9. C
5. C 10. B

TEST 11

DIRECTIONS: Each of questions 1 through 10 consists of four words, one of which may be spelled incorrectly or all four words may be spelled correctly. If one of the words in a question is spelled INCORRECTLY, print in the space at the right the capital letter preceding the word which is spelled incorrectly. If all four words are spelled CORRECTLY, print the letter E.

1. A. vehicular   B. gesticulate   1._____
   C. manageable   D. fullfil

2. A. inovation   B. onerous   2._____
   C. chastise   D. irresistible

3. A. familiarize   B. dissolution   3._____
   C. oscillate   D. superflous

4. A. census   B. defender   4._____
   C. adherence   D. inconceivable

5. A. voluminous   B. liberalize   5._____
   C. bankrupcy   D. conversion

6. A. justifiable   B. executor   6._____
   C. perpatrate   D. dispelled

7. A. boycott   B. abeyence   7._____
   C. enterprise   D. circular

8. A. spontaineous   B. dubious   8._____
   C. analyze   D. premonition

9. A. intelligible   B. apparently   9._____
   C. genuine   D. crucial

10. A. plentiful   B. ascertain   10._____
    C. carreer   D. preliminary

KEY (CORRECT ANSWERS)

1.	D	6.	C
2.	A	7.	B
3.	D	8.	A
4.	E	9.	E
5.	C	10.	C

TEST 12

DIRECTIONS: Each of questions 1 through 25 consists of four words, one of which may be spelled incorrectly or all four words may be spelled correctly. If one of the words in a question is spelled INCORRECTLY, print in the space at the right the capital letter preceding the word which is spelled incorrectly. If all four words are spelled CORRECTLY, print the letter E.

1. A. temporary B. existance C. complimentary D. altogether 1.____

2. A. privilege B. changeable C. jeopardize D. commitment 2.____

3. A. grievous B. alloted C. outrageous D. mortgage 3.____

4. A. tempermental B. accommodating C. bookkeeping D. panicky 4.____

5. A. auxiliary B. indispensable C. ecstasy D. fiery 5.____

6. A. dissappear B. buoyant C. imminent D. parallel 6.____

7. A. loosly B. medicine C. schedule D. defendant 7.____

8. A. endeavor B. persuade C. retroactive D. desparate 8.____

9. A. usage B. servicable C. disadvantageous D. remittance 9.____

10. A. beneficary B. receipt C. excitable D. implement 10.____

11. A. accompanying B. intangible C. offerred D. movable 11.____

12. A. controlling B. seize C. repetitious D. miscellaneous 12.____

13. A. installation B. accommodation C. consistant D. illuminate 13.____

14. A. incidentaly B. privilege C. apparent D. chargeable 14.____

2 (#12)

15. A. prevalent B. serial 15._____
    C. briefly D. disatisfied

16. A. reciprocal B. concurrence 16._____
    C. persistence D. withold

17. A. deferred B. suing 17._____
    C. fulfilled D. pursuant

18. A. questionable B. omission 18._____
    C. acknowledgment D. insistent

19. A. guarantee B. committment 19._____
    C. mitigate D. publicly

20. A. prerogative B. apprise 20._____
    C. extrordinary D. continual

21. A. arrogant B. handicapped 21._____
    C. judicious D. perennial

22. A. permissable B. deceive 22._____
    C. innumerable D. retrieve

23. A. notable B. allegiance 23._____
    C. reimburse D. illegal

24. A. wholly B. disbursement 24._____
    C. hindrance D. conciliatory

25. A. guidance B. condemn 25._____
    C. publically D. coercion

KEY (CORRECT ANSWERS)

1.	B	11.	C
2.	E	12.	E
3.	B	13.	C
4.	A	14.	A
5.	E	15.	D
6.	A	16.	D
7.	A	17.	E
8.	D	18.	A
9.	B	19.	B
10.	A	20.	C

21. E
22. A
23. E
24. E
25. C

READING COMPREHENSION
UNDERSTANDING AND INTERPRETING WRITTEN MATERIAL
EXAMINATION SECTION
TEST 1

DIRECTIONS: Each question or incomplete statement is followed by several suggested answers or completions. Select the one that BEST answers the question or completes the statement. *PRINT THE LETTER OF THE CORRECT ANSWER IN THE SPACE AT THE RIGHT.*

Questions 1-3.

DIRECTIONS: Questions 1 through 3 are to be answered SOLELY on the basis of the following statement.

The equipment in a mailroom may include a mail metering machine. This machine simultaneously stamps, postmarks, seals, and counts letters as fast as the operator can feed them. It can also print the proper postage directly on a gummed strip to be affixed to bulky items. It is equipped with a meter which is removed from the machine and sent to the postmaster to be set for a given number of stampings of any denomination. The setting of the meter must be paid for in advance. One of the advantages of metered mail is that it bypasses the cancellation operation and thereby facilitates handling by the post office. Mail metering also makes the pilfering of stamps impossible, but does not prevent the passage of personal mail in company envelopes through the meters unless there is established a rigid control or censorship over outgoing mail.

1. According to this statement, the postmaster

    A. is responsible for training new clerks in the use of mail metering machines
    B. usually recommends that both large and small firms adopt the use of mail metering machines
    C. is responsible for setting the meter to print a fixed number of stampings
    D. examines the mail metering machine to see that they are properly installed in the mailroom

2. According to this statement, the use of mail metering machines

    A. requires the employment of more clerks in a mailroom than does the use of postage stamps
    B. interferes with the handling of large quantities of outgoing mail
    C. does not prevent employees from sending their personal letters at company expense
    D. usually involves smaller expenditures for mailroom equipment than does the use of postage stamps

3. On the basis of this statement, it is MOST accurate to state that

    A. mail metering machines are often used for opening envelopes
    B. postage stamps are generally used when bulky packages are to be mailed
    C. the use of metered mail tends to interfere with rapid mail handling by the post office
    D. mail metering machines can seal and count letters at the same time

1._____

2._____

3._____

Questions 4-5.

DIRECTIONS: Questions 4 and 5 are to be answered SOLELY on the basis of the following statement.

Forms are printed sheets of paper on which information is to be entered. While what is printed on the form is most important, the kind of paper used in making the form is also important. The kind of paper should be selected with regard to the use to which the form will be subjected. Printing a form on an unnecessarily expensive grade of papers is wasteful. On the other hand, using too cheap or flimsy a form can materially interfere with satisfactory performance of the work the form is being planned to do. Thus, a form printed on both sides normally requires a heavier paper than a form printed only on one side. Forms to be used as permanent records, or which are expected to have a very long life in files, requires a quality of paper which will not disintegrate or discolor with age. A form which will go through a great deal of handling requires a strong, tough paper, while thinness is a necessary qualification where the making of several copies of a form will be required.

4. According to this statement, the type of paper used for making forms

   A. should be chosen in accordance with the use to which the form will be put
   B. should be chosen before the type of printing to be used has been decided upon
   C. is as important as the information which is printed on it
   D. should be strong enough to be used for any purpose

5. According to this statement, forms that are

   A. printed on both sides are usually economical and desirable
   B. to be filed permanently should not deteriorate as time goes on
   C. expected to last for a long time should be handled carefully
   D. to be filed should not be printed on inexpensive paper

Questions 6-8.

DIRECTIONS: Questions 6 through 8 are to be answered SOLELY on the basis of the following paragraph.

The increase in the number of public documents in the last two centuries closely matches the increase in population in the United States. The great number of public documents has become a serious threat to their usefulness. It is necessary to have programs which will reduce the number of public documents that are kept and which will, at the same time, assure keeping those that have value. Such programs need a great deal of thought to have any success.

6. According to the above paragraph, public documents may be LESS useful if

   A. the files are open to the public
   B. the record room is too small
   C. the copying machine is operated only during normal working hours
   D. too many records are being kept

7. According to the above paragraph, the growth of the population in the United States has matched the growth in the quantity of public documents for a period of MOST NEARLY _____ years.

   A. 50   B. 100   C. 200   D. 300

7._____

8. According to the above paragraph, the increased number of public documents has made it necessary to

   A. find out which public documents are worth keeping
   B. reduce the great number of public documents by decreasing government services
   C. eliminate the copying of all original public documents
   D. avoid all new copying devices

8._____

Questions 9-10.

DIRECTIONS: Questions 9 and 10 are to be answered SOLELY on the basis of the following paragraph.

The work goals of an agency can best be reached if the employees understand and agree with these goals. One way to gain such understanding and agreement is for management to encourage and seriously consider suggestions from employees in the setting of agency goals.

9. On the basis of the above paragraph, the BEST way to achieve the work goals of an agency is to

   A. make certain that employees work as hard as possible
   B. study the organizational structure of the agency
   C. encourage employees to think seriously about the agency's problems
   D. stimulate employee understanding of the work goals

9._____

10. On the basis of the above paragraph, understanding and agreement with agency goals can be gained by

    A. allowing the employees to set agency goals
    B. reaching agency goals quickly
    C. legislative review of agency operations
    D. employee participation in setting agency goals

10._____

Questions 11-13.

DIRECTIONS: Questions 11 through 13 are to be answered SOLELY on the basis of the following paragraph.

In order to organize records properly, it is necessary to start from their very beginning and trace each copy of the record to find out how it is used, how long it is used, and what may finally be done with it. Although several copies of the record are made, one copy should be marked as the copy of record. This is the formal legal copy, held to meet the requirements of the law. The other copies may be retained for brief periods for reference purposes, but these copies should not be kept after their usefulness as reference ends. There is another reason for tracing records through the office and that is to determine how long it takes the copy of record to reach the central file. The copy of record must not be kept longer than necessary by the section of the office which has prepared it, but should be sent to the central file as soon as possible so that it can be available to the various sections of the office. The central file can make the copy of record available to the various sections of the office at an early date only if it arrives at the central file as quickly as possible. Just as soon as its immediate or active service period is ended, the copy of record should be removed from the central file and put into the inactive file in the office to be stored for whatever length of time may be necessary to meet legal requirements, and then destroyed.

11. According to the above paragraph, a reason for tracing records through an office is to

   A. determine how long the central file must keep the records
   B. organize records properly
   C. find out how many copies of each record are required
   D. identify the copy of record

12. According to the above paragraph, in order for the central file to have the copy of record available as soon as possible for the various sections of the office, it is MOST important that the

   A. copy of record to be sent to the central file meets the requirements of the law
   B. copy of record is not kept in the inactive file too long
   C. section preparing the copy of record does not unduly delay in sending it to the central file
   D. central file does not keep the copy of record beyond its active service period

13. According to the above paragraph, the length of time a copy of a record is kept in the inactive file of an office depends CHIEFLY on the

   A. requirements of the law
   B. length of time that is required to trace the copy of record through the office
   C. use that is made of the copy of record
   D. length of the period that the copy of record is used for reference purposes

Questions 14-16.

DIRECTIONS: Questions 14 through 16 are to be answered SOLELY on the basis of the following paragraph.

The office was once considered as nothing more than a focal point of internal and external correspondence. It was capable only of dispatching a few letters upon occasion and of preparing records of little practical value. Under such a concept, the vitality of the office force was impaired. Initiative became stagnant, and the lot of the office worker was not likely to be a happy one. However, under the new concept of office management, the possibilities of waste and mismanagement in office operation are now fully recognized, as are the possibilities for the modern office to assist in the direction and control of business operations. Fortunately, the modern concept of the office as a centralized service-rendering unit is gaining ever greater acceptance in today's complex business world, for without the modern office, the production wheels do not turn and the distribution of goods and services is not possible.

14. According to the above paragraph, the fundamental difference between the old and the new concept of the office is the change in the

    A. accepted functions of the office
    B. content and the value of the records kept
    C. office methods and systems
    D. vitality and morale of the office force

14.____

15. According to the above paragraph, an office operated today under the old concept of the office MOST likely would

    A. make older workers happy in their jobs
    B. be part of an old thriving business concern
    C. have a passive role in the conduct of a business enterprise
    D. attract workers who do not believe in modern methods

15.____

16. Of the following, the MOST important implication of the above paragraph is that a present-day business organization cannot function effectively without the

    A. use of modern office equipment
    B. participation and cooperation of the office
    C. continued modernization of office procedures
    D. employment of office workers with skill and initiative

16.____

Questions 17-20.

DIRECTIONS: Questions 17 through 20 are to be answered SOLELY on the basis of the following paragraph.

    A report is frequently ineffective because the person writing it is not fully acquainted with all the necessary details before he actually starts to construct the report. All details pertaining to the subject should be known before the report is started. If the essential facts are not known, they should be investigated. It is wise to have essential facts written down rather than to depend too much on memory, especially if the facts pertain to such matters as amounts, dates, names of persons, or other specific data. When the necessary information has been gathered, the general plan and content of the report should be thought out before the writing is actually begun. A person with little or no experience in writing reports may find that it is wise to make a brief outline. Persons with more experience should not need a written outline, but they should make mental notes of the steps they are to follow. If writing reports without dictation is a regular part of an office worker's duties, he should set aside a certain time during the day when he is least likely to be interrupted. That may be difficult, but in most offices there are certain times in the day when the callers, telephone calls, and other interruptions are not numerous. During those times, it is best to write reports that need undivided concentration. Reports that are written amid a series of interruptions may be poorly done.

17. Before starting to write an effective report, it is necessary to

    A. memorize all specific information
    B. disregard ambiguous data
    C. know all pertinent information
    D. develop a general plan

17.____

18. Reports dealing with complex and difficult material should be

    A. prepared and written by the supervisor of the unit
    B. written when there is the least chance of interruption
    C. prepared and written as part of regular office routine
    D. outlined and then dictated

19. According to the paragraph, employees with no prior familiarity in writing reports may find it helpful to

    A. prepare a brief outline
    B. mentally prepare a synopsis of the report's content
    C. have a fellow employee help in writing the report
    D. consult previous reports

20. In writing a report, needed information which is unclear should be

    A. disregarded   B. memorized
    C. investigated   D. gathered

Questions 21-25.

DIRECTIONS: Questions 21 through 25 are to be answered SOLELY on the basis of the following passage.

Positive discipline minimizes the amount of personal supervision required and aids in the maintenance of standards. When a new employee has been properly introduced and carefully instructed, when he has come to know the supervisor and has confidence in the supervisor's ability to take care of him, when he willingly cooperates with the supervisor, that employee has been under positive discipline and can be put on his own to produce the quantity and quality of work desired. Negative discipline, the fear of transfer to a less desirable location, for example, to a limited extent may restrain certain individuals from overt violation of rules and regulations governing attendance and conduct which in governmental agencies are usually on at least an agency-wide basis. Negative discipline may prompt employees to perform according to certain rules to avoid a penalty such as, for example, docking for tardiness.

21. According to the above passage, it is reasonable to assume that in the area of discipline, the first-line supervisor in a governmental agency has GREATER scope for action in

    A. *positive* discipline, because negative discipline is largely taken care of by agency rules and regulations
    B. *negative* discipline, because rules and procedures are already fixed and the supervisor can rely on them
    C. *positive* discipline, because the supervisor is in a position to recommend transfers
    D. *negative* discipline, because positive discipline is reserved for people on a higher supervisory level

22. In order to maintain positive discipline of employees under his supervision, it is MOST important for a supervisor to

    A. assure each employee that he has nothing to worry about
    B. insist at the outset on complete cooperation from employees

C. be sure that each employee is well trained in his job
D. inform new employees of the penalties for not meeting standards

23. According to the above passage, a feature of negative discipline is that it

   A. may lower employee morale
   B. may restrain employees from disobeying the rules
   C. censures equal treatment of employees
   D. tends to create standards for quality of work

24. A REASONABLE conclusion based on the above passage is that positive discipline benefits a supervisor because

   A. he can turn over orientation and supervision of a new employee to one of his subordinates
   B. subordinates learn to cooperate with one another when working on an assignment
   C. it is easier to administer
   D. it cuts down, in the long run, on the amount of time the supervisor needs to spend on direct supervision

25. Based on the above passage, it is REASONABLE to assume, that an important difference between positive discipline and negative discipline is that positive discipline

   A. is concerned with the quality of work and negative discipline with the quantity of work
   B. leads to a more desirable basis for motivation of the employee
   C. is more likely to be concerned with agency rules and regulations
   D. uses fear while negative discipline uses penalties to prod employees to adequate performance

KEY (CORRECT ANSWERS)

1.	C	11.	B
2.	C	12.	C
3.	D	13.	A
4.	A	14.	A
5.	B	15.	C
6.	D	16.	B
7.	C	17.	C
8.	A	18.	B
9.	D	19.	A
10.	D	20.	B

21. A
22. C
23. B
24. D
25. B

TEST 2

Questions 1-6.

DIRECTIONS: Questions 1 through 6 are to be answered SOLELY on the basis of the following passage.

Inherent in all organized endeavors is the need to resolve the individual differences involved in conflict. Conflict may be either a positive or negative factor since it may lead to creativity, innovation and progress on the one hand, or it may result, on the other hand, in a deterioration or even destruction of the organization. Thus, some forms of conflict are desirable, whereas others are undesirable and ethically wrong.

There are three management strategies which deal with interpersonal conflict. In the *divide-and-rule strategy,* management attempts to maintain control by limiting the conflict to those directly involved and preventing their disagreement from spreading to the larger group. The *suppression-of-differences strategy* entails ignoring conflicts or pretending they are irrelevant. In the *working-through-differences strategy,* management actively attempts to solve or resolve intergroup or interpersonal conflicts. Of the three strategies, only the last directly attacks and has the potential for eliminating the causes of conflict. An essential part of this strategy, however, is its employment by a committed and relatively mature management team.

1. According to the above passage, the *divide-and-rule strategy tor* dealing with conflict is the attempt to

    A. involve other people in the conflict
    B. restrict the conflict to those participating in it
    C. divide the conflict into positive and negative factors
    D. divide the conflict into a number of smaller ones

2. The word *conflict* is used in relation to both positive and negative factors in this passage. Which one of the following words is MOST likely to describe the activity which the word *conflict,* in the sense of the passage, implies?

    A. Competition   B. Confusion
    C. Cooperation   D. Aggression

3. According to the above passage, which one of the following characteristics is shared by both the *suppression-of-differences strategy* and the *divide-and-rule strategy*?

    A. Pretending that conflicts are irrelevant
    B. Preventing conflicts from spreading to the group situation
    C. Failure to directly attack the causes of conflict
    D. Actively attempting to resolve interpersonal conflict

4. According to the above passage, the successful resolution of interpersonal conflict requires

    A. allowing the group to mediate conflicts between two individuals
    B. division of the conflict into positive and negative factors
    C. involvement of a committed, mature management team
    D. ignoring minor conflicts until they threaten the organization

5. Which can be MOST reasonably inferred from the above passage? Conflict between two individuals is LEAST likely to continue when management uses

   A. the *working-through differences strategy*
   B. the *suppression-of differences strategy*
   C. the *divide-and-rule strategy*
   D. a combination of all three strategies

6. According to the above passage, a DESIRABLE result of conflict in an organization is when conflict

   A. exposes production problems in the organization
   B. can be easily ignored by management
   C. results in advancement of more efficient managers
   D. leads to development of new methods

Questions 7-13.

DIRECTIONS: Questions 7 through 13 are to be answered SOLELY on the basis of the passage below.

Modern management places great emphasis on the concept of communication. The communication process consists of the steps through which an idea or concept passes from its inception by one person, the sender, until it is acted upon by another person, the receiver. Through an understanding of these steps and some of the possible barriers that may occur, more effective communication may be achieved. The first step in the communication process is ideation by the sender. This is the formation of the intended content of the message he wants to transmit. In the next step, encoding, the sender organizes his ideas into a series of symbols designed to communicate his message to his intended receiver. He selects suitable words or phrases that can be understood by the receiver, and he also selects the appropriate media to be used—for example, memorandum, conference, etc. The third step is transmission of the encoded message through selected channels in the organizational structure. In the fourth step, the receiver enters the process by tuning in to receive the message. If the receiver does not function, however, the message is lost. For example, if the message is oral, the receiver must be a good listener. The fifth step is decoding of the message by the receiver, as for example, by changing words into ideas. At this step, the decoded message may not be the same idea that the sender originally encoded because the sender and receiver have different perceptions regarding the meaning of certain words. Finally, the receiver acts or responds. He may file the information, ask for more information, or take other action. There can be no assurance, however, that communication has taken place unless there is some type of feedback to the sender in the form of an acknowledgement that the message was received.

7. According to the above passage, *ideation* is the process by which the

   A. sender develops the intended content of the message
   B. sender organizes his ideas into a series of symbols
   C. receiver tunes in to receive the message
   D. receiver decodes the message

8. In the last sentence of the passage, the word *feedback* refers to the process by which the sender is assured that the

    A. receiver filed the information
    B. receiver's perception is the same as his own
    C. message was received
    D. message was properly interpreted

9. Which one of the following BEST shows the order of the steps in the communication process as described in the passage?

    A. 1 - ideation   2 - encoding
       3 - decoding   4 - transmission
       5 - receiving   6 - action
       7 - feedback to the sender

    B. 1 - ideation   2 - encoding
       3 - transmission   4 - decoding
       5 - receiving   6 - action
       7 - feedback to the sender

    C. 1 - ideation   2 - decoding
       3 - transmission   4 - receiving
       5 - encoding   6 - action
       7 - feedback to the sender

    D. 1 - ideation   2 - encoding
       3 - transmission   4 - receiving
       5 - decoding   6 - action
       7 - feedback to the sender

10. Which one of the following BEST expresses the main theme of the passage?

    A. Different individuals have the same perceptions regarding the meaning of words.
    B. An understanding of the steps in the communication process may achieve better communication.
    C. Receivers play a passive role in the communication process.
    D. Senders should not communicate with receivers who transmit feedback.

11. The above passage implies that a receiver does NOT function properly when he

    A. transmits feedback   B. files the information
    C. is a poor listener   D. asks for more information

12. Which one of the following, according to the above passage, is included in the SECOND step of the communication process?

    A. Selecting the appropriate media to be used in transmission
    B. Formulation of the intended content of the message
    C. Using appropriate media to respond to the receiver's feedback
    D. Transmitting the message through selected channels in the organization

13. The above passage implies that the *decoding process* is MOST NEARLY the reverse of the _____ process.

    A. transmission   B. receiving
    C. feedback   D. encoding

Questions 14-19.

DIRECTIONS: Questions 14 through 19 are to be answered SOLELY on the basis of the following passage.

It is often said that no system will work if the people who carry it out do not want it to work. In too many cases, a departmental reorganization that seemed technically sound and economically practical has proved to be a failure because the planners neglected to take the human factor into account. The truth is that employees are likely to feel threatened when they learn that a major change is in the wind. It does not matter whether or not the change actually poses a threat to an employee; the fact that he believes it does or fears it might is enough to make him feel insecure. Among the dangers he fears, the foremost is the possibility that his job may cease to exist and that he may be laid off or shunted into a less skilled position at lower pay. Even if he knows that his own job category is secure, however, he is likely to fear losing some of the important intangible advantages of his present position—for instance, he may fear that he will be separated from his present companions and thrust in with a group of strangers, or that he will find himself in a lower position on the organizational ladder if a new position is created above his.

It is important that management recognize these natural fears and take them into account in planning any kind of major change. While there is no cut-and-dried formula for preventing employee resistance, there are several steps that can be taken to reduce employees' fears and gain their cooperation. First, unwarranted fears can be dispelled if employees are kept informed of the planning from the start and if they know exactly what to expect. Next, assurance on matters such as retraining, transfers, and placement help should be given as soon as it is clear what direction the reorganization will take. Finally, employees' participation in the planning should be actively sought. There is a great psychological difference between feeling that a change is being forced upon one from the outside, and feeling that one is an insider who is helping to bring about a change.

14. According to the above passage, employees who are not in real danger of losing their jobs because of a proposed reorganization

    A. will be eager to assist in the reorganization
    B. will pay little attention to the reorganization
    C. should not be taken into account in planning the reorganization
    D. are nonetheless likely to feel threatened by the reorganization

15. The passage mentions the *intangible advantages* of a position.
    Which of the following BEST describes the kind of advantages alluded to in the passage?

    A. Benefits such as paid holidays and vacations
    B. Satisfaction of human needs for things like friendship and status
    C. Qualities such as leadership and responsibility
    D. A work environment that meets satisfactory standards of health and safety

16. According to the passage, an employee's fear that a reorganization may separate him from his present companions is a (n)

    A. childish and immature reaction to change
    B. unrealistic feeling since this is not going to happen

C. possible reaction that the planners should be aware of
D. incentive to employees to participate in the planning

17. On the basis of the above passage, it would be DESIRABLE, when planning a departmental reorganization, to   17._____

    A. be governed by employee feelings and attitudes
    B. give some employees lower positions
    C. keep employees informed
    D. lay off those who are less skilled

18. What does the passage say can be done to help gain employees' cooperation in a reorganization?   18._____

    A. Making sure that the change is technically sound, that it is economically practical, and that the human factor is taken into account
    B. Keeping employees fully informed, offering help in fitting them into new positions, and seeking their participation in the planning
    C. Assuring employees that they will not be laid off, that they will not be reassigned to a group of strangers, and that no new positions will be created on the organization ladder
    D. Reducing employees' fears, arranging a retraining program, and providing for transfers

19. Which of the following suggested titles would be MOST appropriate for this passage?   19._____

    A. PLANNING A DEPARTMENTAL REORGANIZATION
    B. WHY EMPLOYEES ARE AFRAID
    C. LOOKING AHEAD TO THE FUTURE
    D. PLANNING FOR CHANGE: THE HUMAN FACTOR

Questions 20-22.

DIRECTIONS: Questions 20 through 22 are to be answered SOLELY on the basis of the following passage.

The achievement of good human relations is essential if a business office is to produce at top efficiency and is to be a pleasant place in which to work. All office workers plan an important role in handling problems in human relations. They should, therefore, strive to acquire the understanding, tactfulness, and awareness necessary to deal effectively with actual office situations involving co-workers on all levels. Only in this way can they truly become responsible, interested, cooperative, and helpful members of the staff.

20. The selection implies that the MOST important value of good human relations in an office is to develop   20._____

    A. efficiency   B. cooperativeness
    C. tact   D. pleasantness and efficiency

21. Office workers should acquire understanding in dealing with   21._____

    A. co-workers   B. subordinates
    C. superiors   D. all members of the staff

6 (#2)

22. The selection indicates that a highly competent secretary who is also very argumentative is meeting office requirements   22.____

   A. wholly
   B. partly
   C. slightly
   D. not at all

Questions 23-25.

DIRECTIONS: Questions 23 through 25 are to be answered SOLELY on the basis of the following passage.

It is common knowledge that ability to do a particular job and performance on the job do not always go hand in hand. Persons with great potential abilities sometimes fall down on the job because of laziness or lack of interest in the job, while persons with mediocre talents have often achieved excellent results through their industry and their loyalty to the interests of their employers. It is clear; therefore, that in a balanced personnel program, measures of employee ability need to be supplemented by measures of employee performance, for the final test of any employee is his performance on the job.

23. The MOST accurate of the following statements, on the basis of the above paragraph, is that   23.____

   A. employees who lack ability are usually not industrious
   B. an employee's attitudes are more important than his abilities
   C. mediocre employees who are interested in their work are preferable to employees who possess great ability
   D. superior capacity for performance should be supplemented with proper attitudes

24. On the basis of the above paragraph, the employee of most value to his employer is NOT necessarily the one who   24.____

   A. best understands the significance of his duties
   B. achieves excellent results
   C. possesses the greatest talents
   D. produces the greatest amount of work

25. According to the above paragraph, an employee's efficiency is BEST determined by an   25.____

   A. appraisal of his interest in his work
   B. evaluation of the work performed by him
   C. appraisal of his loyalty to his employer
   D. evaluation of his potential ability to perform his work

7 (#2)

KEY (CORRECT ANSWERS)

1.	B	11.	C
2.	A	12.	A
3.	C	13.	D
4.	C	14.	D
5.	A	15.	B
6.	D	16.	C
7.	A	17.	C
8.	C	18.	B
9.	D	19.	D
10.	B	20.	D

21. D
22. B
23. D
24. C
25. B

———

TEST 3

Questions 1-8.

DIRECTIONS: Questions 1 through 8 are to be answered SOLELY on the basis of the following information and directions.

Assume that you are a clerk in a city agency. Your supervisor has asked you to classify each of the accidents that happened to employees in the agency into the following five categories:

   A. An accident that occurred in the period from January through June, between 9 A.M. and 12 Noon, that was the result of carelessness on the part of the injured employee, that caused the employee to lose less than seven working hours, that happened to an employee who was 40 years of age or over, and who was employed in the agency for less than three years;

   B. An accident that occurred in the period from July through December, after 1 P.M., that was the result of unsafe conditions, that caused the injured employee to lose less than seven working hours, that happened to an employee who was 40 years of age or over, and who was employed in the agency for three years or more;

   C. An accident that occurred in the period from January through June, after 1 P.M., that was the result of carelessness on the part of the injured employee, that caused the injured employee to lose seven or more working hours, that happened to an employee who was less than 40 years old, and who was employed in the agency for three years or more;

   D. An accident that occurred in the period from July through December, between 9 A.M. and 12 Noon, that was the result of unsafe conditions, that caused the injured employee to lose seven or more working hours, that happened to an employee who was less than 40 years old, and who was employed in the agency for less than three years;

   E. Accidents that cannot be classified in any of the foregoing groups. NOTE: In classifying these accidents, an employee's age and length of service are computed as of the date of accident. In all cases, it is to be assumed that each employee has been employed continuously in city service, and that each employee works seven hours a day, from 9 A.M. to 5 P.M., with lunch from 12 Noon to 1 P.M. In each question, consider only the information which will assist you in classifying the accident. Any information which is of no assistance in classifying an accident should not be considered.

1. The unsafe condition of the stairs in the building caused Miss Perkins to have an accident on October 14, 2003 at 4 P.M. When she returned to work the following day at 1 P.M., Miss Perkins said that the accident was the first one that had occurred to her in her ten years of employment with the agency. She was born on April 27, 1962.   1._____

2. On the day after she completed her six-month probationary period of employment with the agency, Miss Green, who had been considered a careful worker by her supervisor, injured her left foot in an accident caused by her own carelessness. She went home immediately after the accident, which occurred at 10 A.M., March 19, 2004, but returned to work at the regular time on the following morning. Miss Green was born July 12, 1963 in New York City.   2._____

3. The unsafe condition of a duplicating machine caused Mr. Martin to injure himself in an accident on September 8, 2006 at 2 P.M. As a result of the accident, he was unable to work the remainder of the day, but returned to his office ready for work on the following morning. Mr. Martin, who has been working for the agency since April 1, 2003, was born in St. Louis on February 1, 1968. 3.____

4. Mr. Smith was hospitalized for two weeks because of a back injury resulted from an accident on the morning of November 16, 2006. Investigation of the accident revealed that it was caused by the unsafe condition of the floor on which Mr. Smith had been walking. Mr. Smith, who is an accountant, has been anemployee of the agency since March 1, 2004, and was born in Ohio on June 10, 1968. 4.____

5. Mr. Allen cut his right hand because he was careless in operating a multilith machine. Mr. Allen, who was 33 years old when the accident took place, has been employed by the agency since August 17, 1992. The accident, which occurred on January 26, 2006, at 2 P.M., caused Mr. Allen to be absent from work for the rest of the day. He was able to return to work the next morning. 5.____

6. Mr. Rand, who is a college graduate, was born on December, 28, 1967, and has been working for the agency since January 7, 2002. On Monday, April 25, 2005, at 2 P.M., his carelessness in operating a duplicating machine caused him to have an accident and to be sent home from work immediately. Fortunately, he was able to return to work at his regular time on the following Wednesday. 6.____

7. Because he was careless in running down a flight of stairs, Mr. Brown fell, bruising his right hand. Although the accident occurred shortly after he arrived for work on the morning of May 22, 2006, he was unable to resume work until 3 P.M. that day. Mr. Brown was born on August 15, 1955, and began working for the agency on September 12, 2003, as a clerk, at a salary of $22,750 per annum. 7.____

8. On December 5, 2005, four weeks after he had begun working for the agency, the unsafe condition of an automatic stapling machine caused Mr. Thomas to injure himself in an accident. Mr. Thomas, who was born on May 19,1975, lost three working days because of the accident, which occurred at 11:45 A.M. 8.____

Questions 9-10.

DIRECTIONS: Questions 9 and 10 are to be answered SOLELY on the basis of the following paragraph.

An impending reorganization within an agency will mean loss by transfer of several professional staff members from the personnel division. The division chief is asked to designate the persons to be transferred. After reviewing the implications of this reduction of staff with his assistant, the division chief discusses the matter at a staff meeting. He adopts the recommendations of several staff members to have volunteers make up the required reduction.

9. The decision to permit personnel to volunteer for transfer is

   A. *poor;* it is not likely that the members of a division are of equal value to the division chief
   B. *good;* dissatisfied members will probably be more productive elsewhere
   C. *poor;* the division chief has abdicated his responsibility to carry out the order given to him
   D. *good;* morale among remaining staff is likely to improve in a more cohesive framework

10. Suppose that one of the volunteers is a recently appointed employee who has completed his probationary period acceptably, but whose attitude toward division operations and agency administration tends to be rather negative and sometimes even abrasive. Because of his lack of commitment to the division, his transfer is recommended. If the transfer is approved, the division chief should, prior to the transfer,

    A. discuss with the staff the importance of commitment to the work of the agency and its relationship with job satisfaction
    B. refrain from any discussion of attitude with the employee
    C. discuss with the employee his concern about the employee's attitude
    D. avoid mention of attitude in the evaluation appraisal prepared for the receiving division chief

Questions 11-16.

DIRECTIONS: Questions 11 through 16 are to be answered SOLELY on the basis of the following paragraph.

Methods of administration of office activities, much of which consists of providing information and *know-how* needed to coordinate both activities within that particular office and other offices, have been among the last to come under the spotlight of management analysis. Progress has been rapid during the past decade, however, and is now accelerating at such a pace that an *information revolution* in office management appears to be in the making. Although triggered by technological breakthroughs in electronic computers and other giant steps in mechanization, this information revolution must be attributed to underlying forces, such as the increased complexity of both governmental and private enterprise, and ever-keener competition. Size, diversification, specialization of function, and decentralization are among the forces which make coordination of activities both more imperative and more difficult. Increased competition, both domestic and international, leaves little margin for error in managerial decisions. Several developments during recent years indicate an evolving pattern. In 1960, the American Management Association expanded the scope of its activities and changed the name of its Office Management Division to Administrative Services Division. Also in 1960, the magazine *Office Management* merged with the magazine *American Business,* and this new publication was named *Administrative Management.*

11. A REASONABLE inference that can be made from the information in the above paragraph is that an important role of the office manager today is to

    A. work toward specialization of functions performed by his subordinates
    B. inform and train subordinates regarding any new developments in computer technology and mechanization
    C. assist the professional management analysts with the management analysis work in the organization
    D. supply information that can be used to help coordinate and manage the other activities of the organization

12. An IMPORTANT reason for the *information revolution* that has been taking place in office management is the

    A. advance made in management analysis in the past decade
    B. technological breakthrough in electronic computers and mechanization
    C. more competitive and complicated nature of private business and government
    D. increased efficiency of office management techniques in the past ten years

13. According to the above paragraph, specialization of function in an organization is MOST likely to result in

    A. the elimination of errors in managerial decisions
    B. greater need to coordinate activities
    C. more competition with other organizations, both domestic and international
    D. a need for office managers with greater flexibility

14. The word *evolving,* as used in the third from last sentence in the above paragraph, means MOST NEARLY

    A. developing by gradual changes
    B. passing on to others
    C. occurring periodically
    D. breaking up into separate, constituent parts

15. Of the following, the MOST reasonable implication of the changes in names mentioned in the last part of the above paragraph is that these groups are attempting to

    A. professionalize the field of office management and the title of Office Manager
    B. combine two publications into one because of the increased costs of labor and materials
    C. adjust to the fact that the field of office management is broadening
    D. appeal to the top managerial people rather than the office management people in business and government

16. According to the above paragraph, intense competition among domestic and international enterprises makes it MOST important for an organization's managerial staff to

    A. coordinate and administer office activities with other activities in the organization
    B. make as few errors in decision-making as possible
    C. concentrate on decentralization and reduction of size of the individual divisions of the organization
    D. restrict decision-making only to top management officials

Questions 17-21.

DIRECTIONS: Questions 17 through 21 are to be answered SOLELY on the basis of the following passage.

For some office workers, it is useful to be familiar with the four main classes of domestic mail; for others, it is essential. Each class has a different rate of postage, and some have requirements concerning wrapping, sealing, or special information to be placed on the package. First class mail, the class which may not be opened for postal inspection, includes letters, postcards, business reply cards, and other kinds of written matter. There are different rates for some of the kinds of cards which can be sent by first class mail. The maximum weight for an item sent by first class mail is 70 pounds. An item which is not letter size should be marked *First Class* on all sides. Although office workers most often come into contact with first class mail, they may find it helpful to know something about the other classes. Second class mail is generally used for mailing newspapers and magazines. Publishers of these articles must meet certain U.S. Postal Service requirements in order to obtain a permit to use second class mailing rates. Third class mail, which must weigh less than 1 pound, includes printed materials and merchandise parcels. There are two rate structures for this class - a single piece rate and a bulk rate. Fourth class mail, also known as parcel post, includes packages weighing from one to 40 pounds. For more information about these classes of mail and the actual mailing rates, contact your local post office.

17. According to this passage, first class mail is the *only* class which

    A. has a limit on the maximum weight of an item
    B. has different rates for items within the class
    C. may not be opened for postal inspection
    D. should be used by office workers

18. According to this passage, the one of the following items which may CORRECTLY be sent by fourth class mail is a

    A. magazine weighing one-half pound
    B. package weighing one-half pound
    C. package weighing two pounds
    D. postcard

19. According to this passage, there are different postage rates for

    A. a newspaper sent by second class mail and a magazine sent by second class mail
    B. each of the classes of mail
    C. each pound of fourth class mail
    D. printed material sent by third class mail and merchandise parcels sent by third class mail

20. In order to send a newspaper by second class mail, a publisher MUST

    A. have met certain postal requirements and obtained a permit
    B. indicate whether he wants to use the single piece or the bulk rate
    C. make certain that the newspaper weighs less than one pound
    D. mark the newspaper *Second Class* on the top and bottom of the wrapper

21. Of the following types of information, the one which is NOT mentioned in the passage is the

    A. class of mail to which parcel post belongs
    B. kinds of items which can be sent by each class of mail
    C. maximum weight for an item sent by fourth class mail
    D. postage rate for each of the four classes of mail

Questions 22-25.

DIRECTIONS: Questions 22 through 25 are to be answered SOLELY on the basis of the following paragraph.

A standard comprises characteristics attached to an aspect of a process or product by which it can be evaluated. Standardization is the development and adoption of standards. When they are formulated, standards are not usually the product of a single person, but represent the thoughts and ideas of a group, leavened with the knowledge and information which are currently available. Standards which do not meet certain basic requirements become a hindrance rather than an aid to progress. Standards must not only be correct, accurate, and precise in requiring no more and no less than what is needed for satisfactory results, but they must also be workable in the sense that their usefulness is not nullified by external conditions. Standards should also be acceptable to the people who use them. If they are not acceptable, they cannot be considered to be satisfactory, although they may possess all the other essential characteristics.

22. According to the above paragraph, a processing standard that requires the use of materials that cannot be procured is MOST likely to be

    A. incomplete   B. unworkable
    C. inaccurate   D. unacceptable

23. According to the above paragraph, the construction of standards to which the performance of job duties should conform is MOST often

    A. the work of the people responsible for seeing that the duties are properly performed
    B. accomplished by the person who is best informed about the functions involved
    C. the responsibility of the people who are to apply them
    D. attributable to the efforts of various informed persons

24. According to the above paragraph, when standards call for finer tolerances than those essential to the conduct of successful production operations, the effect of the standards on the improvement of production operations is

    A. negative   B. negligible
    C. nullified   D. beneficial

25. The one of the following which is the MOST suitable title for the above paragraph is

    A. THE EVALUATION OF FORMULATED STANDARDS
    B. THE ATTRIBUTES OF SATISFACTORY STANDARDS
    C. THE ADOPTION OF ACCEPTABLE STANDARDS
    D. THE USE OF PROCESS OR PRODUCT STANDARDS

KEY (CORRECT ANSWERS)

1.	B	11.	D
2.	A	12.	C
3.	E	13.	B
4.	D	14.	A
5.	E	15.	C
6.	C	16.	B
7.	A	17.	C
8.	D	18.	C
9.	A	19.	B
10.	C	20.	A

21. D
22. C
23. D
24. A
25. B

RECORD KEEPING
EXAMINATION SECTION
TEST 1

DIRECTIONS: Each question or incomplete statement is followed by several suggested answers or completions. Select the one that BEST answers the question or completes the statement. *PRINT THE LETTER OF THE CORRECT ANSWER IN THE SPACE AT THE RIGHT.*

Questions 1-15.

DIRECTIONS: Questions 1 through 15 are to be answered on the basis of the following list of company names below. Arrange a file alphabetically, word-by-word, disregarding punctuation, conjunctions, and apostrophes. Then answer the questions.

    A Bee C Reading Materials
    ABCO Parts
    A Better Course for Test Preparation
    AAA Auto Parts Co.
    A-Z Auto Parts, Inc.
    Aabar Books
    Abbey, Joanne
    Boman-Sylvan Law Firm
    BMW Autowerks
    C Q Service Company
    Chappell-Murray, Inc.
    E&E Life Insurance
    Emcrisco
    Gigi Arts
    Gordon, Jon & Associates
    SOS Plumbing
    Schmidt, J.B. Co.

1. Which of these files should appear FIRST?
   A. ABCO Parts
   B. A Bee C Reading Materials
   C. A Better Course for Test Preparation
   D. AAA Auto Parts Co.

1.____

2. Which of these files should appear SECOND?
   A. A-Z Auto Parts, Inc.
   B. A Bee C Reading Materials
   C. A Better Course for Test Preparation
   D. AAA Auto Parts Co.

2.____

3. Which of these files should appear THIRD?
   A. ABCO Parts
   B. A Bee C Reading Materials
   C. Aabar Books
   D. AAA Auto Parts Co.

4. Which of these files should appear FOURTH?
   A. Aabar Books
   B. ABCO Parts
   C. Abbey, Joanne
   D. AAA Auto Parts Co.

5. Which of these files should appear LAST?
   A. Gordon, Jon & Associates
   B. Gigi Arts
   C. Schmidt, J.B. Co.
   D. SOS Plumbing

6. Which of these files should appear between A-Z Auto Parts, Inc. and Abbey, Joanne?
   A. A Bee C Reading Materials
   B. AAA Auto Parts Co.
   C. ABCO Parts
   D. A Better Course for Test Preparation

7. Which of these files should appear between ABCO Parts and Aabar Books?
   A. A Bee C Reading Materials
   B. Abbey, Joanne
   C. Aabar Books
   D. A-Z Auto Parts

8. Which of these files should appear between Abbey, Joanne and Boman-Sylvan Law Firm?
   A. A Better Course for Test Preparation
   B. BMW Autowerks
   C. Chappell-Murray, Inc.
   D. Aabar Books

9. Which of these files should appear between Abbey, Joanne and C Q Service?
   A. A-Z Auto Parts, Inc.
   B. BMW Autowerks
   C. Choices A and B
   D. Chappell-Murray, Inc.

10. Which of these files should appear between C Q Service Company and Emcrisco?
    A. Chappell-Murray, Inc.
    B. E&E Life Insurance
    C. Gigi Arts
    D. Choices A and B

11. Which of these files should NOT appear between C Q Service Company and E&E Life Insurance?
    A. Gordon, Jon & Associates
    B. Emcrisco
    C. Gigi Arts
    D. All of the above

12. Which of these files should appear between Chappell-Murray, Inc. and Gigi Arts?
    A. C Q Service Inc., E&E Life Insurance, and Emcrisco
    B. Emcrisco, E&E Life Insurance, and Gordon, Jon & Associates
    C. E&E Life Insurance, and Emcrisco
    D. Emcrisco and Gordon, Jon & Associates

13. Which of these files should appear between Gordon, Jon & Associates and SOS Plumbing?
    A. Gigi Arts
    B. Schmidt, J.B. Co.
    C. Choices A and B
    D. None of the above

14. Each of the choices lists the four files in their proper alphabetical order EXCEPT
    A. E&E Life Insurance; Gigi Arts; Gordon, Jon & Associates; SOS Plumbing
    B. E&E Life Insurance; Emcrisco; Gigi Arts; SOS Plumbing
    C. Emcrisco; Gordon, Jon & Associates; SOS Plumbing; Schmidt, J.B. Co.
    D. Emcrisco; Gigi Arts; Gordon, Jon & Associates; SOS Plumbing

15. Which of the choices lists the four files in their proper alphabetical order?
    A. Gigi Arts; Gordon, Jon & Associates; SOS Plumbing; Schmidt, J.B. Co.
    B. Gordon, Jon & Associates; Gigi Arts; Schmidt, J.B. Co.; SOS Plumbing
    C. Gordon, Jon & Associates; Gigi Arts; SOS Plumbing; Schmidt, J.B. Co.
    D. Gigi Arts; Gordon, Jon & Associates; Schmidt, J.B. Co.; SOS Plumbing

16. The alphabetical filing order of two businesses with identical names is determined by the
    A. length of time each business has been operating
    B. addresses of the businesses
    C. last name of the company president
    D. no one of the above

17. In an alphabetical filing system, if a business name includes a number, it should be
    A. disregarded
    B. considered a number and placed at the end of an alphabetical section
    C. treated as though it were written in words and alphabetized accordingly
    D. considered a number and placed at the beginning of an alphabetical section

18. If a business name includes a contraction (such as *don't* or *it's*), how should that word be treated in an alphabetical system?
    A. Divide the word into its separate parts and treat it as two words
    B. Ignore the letters that come after the apostrophe
    C. Ignore the word that contains the contraction
    D. Ignore the apostrophe and consider all letters in the contraction

19. In what order should the parts of an address be considered when using an alphabetical filing system?   19._____
    A. City or town; state; street name; house or building number
    B. State; city or town; street name; house or building number
    C. House or building number; street name; city or town; state
    D. Street name; city or town; state

20. A business record should be cross-referenced when a(n)   20._____
    A. organization is known by an abbreviated name
    B. business has a name change because of a sale, incorporation, or other reason
    C. business is known by a *coined* or common name which differs from a dictionary spelling
    D. all of the above

21. A geographical filing system is MOST effective when   21._____
    A. location is more important than name
    B. many names or titles sound alike
    C. dealing with companies who have offices all over the world
    D. filing personal and business files

Questions 22-25.

DIRECTIONS: Questions 22 through 25 are to be answered on the basis of the list of items below, which are to be filed geographically. Organize the items geographically and then answer the questions.

    I. University Press at Berkeley, U.S.
    II. Maria Sanchez, Mexico City, Mexico
    III. Great Expectations Ltd. in London, England
    IV. Justice League, Cape Town, South Africa, Africa
    V. Crown Pearls Ltd. in London, England
    VI. Joseph Prasad in London, England

22. Which of the following arrangements of the items is composed according to the policy of: *Continent, Country, City, Firm or Individual Name*?   22._____
    A. V, III, IV, VI, II, I   B. IV, V, III, VI, II, I
    C. I, IV, V, III, VI, II   D. IV, V, III, VI, I, II

23. Which of the following files is arranged according to the policy of: *Continent, Country, City, Firm or Individual Name*?   23._____
    A. South Africa; Africa; Cape Town; Justice League
    B. Mexico; Mexico City; Maria Sanchez
    C. North America; United States; Berkeley; University Press
    D. England; Europe; London; Prasad, Joseph

24. Which of the following arrangements of the items is composed according to the   24._____
    policy of: *Country, City, Firm or Individual Name*?
    A. V, VI, III, II, IV, I
    B. I, V, VI, III, II, IV
    C. VI, V, III, II, IV, I
    D. V, III, VI, II, IV, I

25. Which of the following files is arranged according to a policy of: *Country,*   25._____
    City, Firm or Individual Name?
    A. England; London; Crown Pearls Ltd.
    B. North America; United States; Berkeley; University Press
    C. Africa; Cape Town; Justice League
    D. Mexico City; Mexico; Maria Sanchez

26. Under which of the following circumstances would a phonetic filing system be   26._____
    MOST effective?
    A. When the person in charge of filing can't spell very well
    B. With large files with names that sound alike
    C. With large files with names that are spelled alike
    D. All of the above

Questions 27-29.

DIRECTIONS: Questions 27 through 29 are to be answered on the basis of the following list of numerical files.

    I.   391-023-100
    II. 361-132-170
    III. 385-732-200
    IV. 381-432-150
    V.   391-632-387
    VI. 361-423-303
    VII. 391-123-271

27. Which of the following arrangements of the files follows a consecutive-digit   27._____
    system?
    A. II, III, IV, I   B. I, V, VII, III   C. II, IV, III, I   D. III, I, V, VII

28. Which of the following arrangements follows a terminal-digit system?   28._____
    A. I, VII, II, IV, III
    B. II, I, IV, V, VII
    C. VII, VI, V, IV, III
    D. I, IV, II, III, VII

29. Which of the following lists follows a middle-digit system?   29._____
    A. I, VII, II, VI, IV, V, III
    B. I, II, VII, IV, VI, V, III
    C. VII, II, I, III, V, VI, IV
    D. VII, I, II, IV, VI, V, III

Questions 30-31.

DIRECTIONS: Questions 30 and 31 are to be answered on the basis of the following information.

   I. Reconfirm Laura Bates appointment with James Caldecort on December 12 at 9:30 A.M.
   II. Laurence Kinder contact Julia Lucas on August 3 and set up a meeting for week of September 23 at 4 P.M.
   III. John Lutz contact Larry Waverly on August 3 and set up appointment for September 23 at 9:30 A.M.
   IV. Call for tickets for Gerry Stanton August 21 for New Jersey on September 23, flight 143 at 4:43 P.M.

30. A chronological file for the above information would be 30.____
   A. IV, III, II, I   B. III, II, IV, I   C. IV, II, III, I   D. III, I, II, IV

31. Using the above information, a chronological file for the date September 23 would be 31.____
   A. II, III, IV   B. III, I, IV   C. III, II, IV   D. IV, III, II

Questions 32-34.

DIRECTIONS: Questions 32 through 34 are to be answered on the basis of the following information.

   I. Call Roger Epstein, Ashoke Naipaul, Jon Anderson, and Sara Washingon on April 19 at 1:00 P.M. to set up meeting with Alika D'Ornay for June 6 in New York.
   II. Call Martin Ames before noon on April 19 to confirm afternoon meeting with Bob Greenwood on April 20th.
   III. Set up meeting room at noon for 2:30 P.M. meeting on April 19th.
   IV. Ashley Stanton contact Bob Greenwood at 9:00 A.M. on April 20 and set up meeting for June 6 at 8:30 A.M.
   V. Carol Guiland contact Shelby Van Ness during afternoon of April 20 and set up meeting for June 6 at 10:00 A.M.
   VI. Call airline and reserve tickets on June 6 for Roger Epstein trip to Denver on July 8.
   VII. Meeting at 2:30 P.M. on April 19th.

32. A chronological file for all of the above information would be 32.____
   A. II, I, III, VII, V, IV, VI
   B. III, VII, II, I, IV, V, VI
   C. III, VII, I, II, V, IV, VI
   D. II, III, I, VII, IV, V, VI

33. A chronological file for the date of April 19th would be 33.____
   A. II, III, VII, I   B. II, III, I, VII   C. VII, I, III, II   D. III, VII, I, II

34. Add the following information to the file, and then create a chronological file for April 20th: VIII. April 20: 3:00 P.M. meeting between Bob Greenwood and Martin Ames.   34.____
    A. IV, V, VIII   B. IV, VIII, V   C. VIII, V, IV   D. V, IV, VIII

35. The PRIMARY advantage of computer records over a manual system is   35.____
    A. speed of retrieval   B. accuracy
    C. cost   D. potential file loss

KEY (CORRECT ANSWERS)

1. B	11. D	21. A	31. C
2. C	12. C	22. B	32. D
3. D	13. B	23. C	33. B
4. A	14. C	24. D	34. A
5. D	15. D	25. A	35. A
6. C	16. B	26. B	
7. B	17. C	27. C	
8. B	18. D	28. D	
9. C	19. A	29. A	
10. D	20. D	30. B	

CLERICAL ABILITIES TEST
EXAMINATION SECTION
TEST 1

DIRECTIONS: Each question or incomplete statement is followed by several suggested answers or completions. Select the one that BEST answers the question or completes the statement. *PRINT THE LETTER OF THE CORRECT ANSWER IN THE SPACE AT THE RIGHT.*

Questions 1-10.

DIRECTIONS: Questions 1 through 10 consist of lines of names, dates, and numbers. For each question, you are to choose the option (A, B, C, or D) in Column II which EXACTLY matches the information in Column I. *PRINT THE LETTER OF THE CORRECT ANSWER IN THE SPACE AT THE RIGHT.*

SAMPLE QUESTION

Column I
Schneider 11/16/75 581932

Column II
A. Schneider 11/16/75 518932
B. Schneider 11/16/75 581932
C. Schnieder 11/16/75 581932
D. Shnieder   11/16/75 518932

The correct answer is B. Only Option B shows the name, date, and number exactly as they are in Column I. Option A has a mistake in the number. Option C has a mistake in the name. Option D has a mistake in the name and in the number. Now answer Questions 1 through 10 in the same manner.

Column I
1. Johnston 12/26/74 659251

Column II
A. Johnson   12/23/74 659251
B. Johston   12/26/74 659251
C. Johnston 12/26/74 695251
D. Johnston 12/26/74 659251

1.____

2. Allison 1/26/75 9939256

A. Allison 1/26/75 9939256
B. Alisson 1/26/75 9939256
C. Allison 1/26/76 9399256
D. Allison 1/26/75 9993356

2.____

3. Farrell 2/12/75 361251

A. Farell   2/21/75 361251
B. Farrell 2/12/75 361251
C. Farrell 2/21/75 361251
D. Farrell 2/12/75 361151

3.____

4. Guerrero 4/28/72 105689
    A. Guererro 4/28/72 105689
    B. Guererro 4/28/72 105986
    C. Guererro 4/28/72 105869
    D. Guerrero 4/28/72 105689

    4.____

5. McDonnell 6/05/73 478215
    A. McDonnell 6/15/73 478215
    B. McDonnell 6/05/73 478215
    C. McDonnell 6/05/73 472815
    D. MacDonell 6/05/73 478215

    5.____

6. Shepard 3/31/71 075421
    A. Sheperd 3/31/71 075421
    B. Shepard 3/13/71 075421
    C. Shepard 3/31/71 075421
    D. Shepard 3/13/71 075241

    6.____

7. Russell 4/01/69 031429
    A. Russell 4/01/69 031429
    B. Russell 4/10/69 034129
    C. Russell 4/10/69 031429
    D. Russell 4/01/69 034129

    7.____

8. Phillips 10/16/68 961042
    A. Philipps 10/16/68 961042
    B. Phillips 10/16/68 960142
    C. Phillips 10/16/68 961042
    D. Philipps 10/16/68 916042

    8.____

9. Campbell 11/21/72 624856
    A. Campbell 11/21/72 624856
    B. Campbell 11/21/72 624586
    C. Campbell 11/21/72 624686
    D. Campbel 11/21/72 624856

    9.____

10. Patterson 9/18/71 76199176
    A. Patterson 9/18/72 76191976
    B. Patterson 9/18/71 76199176
    C. Patterson 9/18/72 76199176
    D. Patterson 9/18/71 76919176

    10.____

Questions 11-15.

DIRECTIONS: Questions 11 through 15 consist of groups of numbers and letters which you are to compare. For each question, you are to choose the option (A, B, C, or D) in Column I which EXACTLY matches the group of numbers and letters given in Column I.

SAMPLE QUESTION

Column I
B92466

Column II
A. B92644
B. B94266
C. A92466
D. B92466

The correct answer is D. Only Option D in Column II shows the group of numbers and letters EXACTLY as it appears in Column I. Now answer Questions 11 through 15 in the same manner.

	Column I		Column II	
11.	925AC5	A.	952CA5	11.____
		B.	925AC5	
		C.	952AC5	
		D.	925CA6	
12.	Y006925	A.	Y060925	12.____
		B.	Y006295	
		C.	Y006529	
		D.	Y006925	
13.	J236956	A.	J236956	13.____
		B.	J326965	
		C.	J239656	
		D.	J932656	
14.	AB6952	A.	AB6952	14.____
		B.	AB9625	
		C.	AB9652	
		D.	AB6925	
15.	X259361	A.	X529361	15.____
		B.	X259631	
		C.	X523961	
		D.	X259361	

Questions 16-25.

DIRECTIONS: Each of questions 16 through 25 consists of three lines of code letters and three lines of numbers. The numbers on each line should correspond with the code letters on the same line in accordance with the table below.

Code Letter	S	V	W	A	Q	M	X	E	G	K
Corresponding Number	0	1	2	3	4	5	5	7	8	9

On some of the lines, an error exists in the coding. Compare the letters and numbers in each question carefully. If you find an error or errors on:
  only one of the lines in the question, mark your answer A;
  any two lines in the question, mark your answer B;
  all three lines in the question, mark your answer C;
  none of the lines in the question, mark your answer D.

SAMPLE QUESTION

WQGKSXG	2489068
XEKVQMA	6591453
KMAESXV	9527061

In the above sample, the first line is correct since each code letter listed has the correct corresponding number. On the second line, an error exists because code letter E should have the number 7 instead of the number 5. On the third line, an error exists because the code letter A should have the number 3 instead of the number 2. Since there are errors in two of the three lines, the correct answer is B. Now answer Questions 16 through 25 in the same manner.

16. SWQEKGA   0247983   16.____
     KEAVSXM   9731065
     SSAXGKQ   0036894

17. QAMKMVS   4259510   17.____
     MGGEASX   5897306
     KSWMKWS   9125920

18. WKXQWVE   2964217   18.____
     QKXXQVA   4966413
     AWMXGVS   3253810

19. GMMKASE   8559307   19.____
     AWVSKSW   3210902
     QAVSVGK   4310189

20. XGKQSMK   6894049   20.____
     QSVKEAS   4019730
     GSMXKMV   8057951

21. AEKMWSG   3195208   21.____
     MKQSVQK   5940149
     XGQAEVW   6843712

22. XGMKAVS   6858310   22.____
     SKMAWEQ   0953174
     GVMEQSA   8167403

23. VQSKAVE   1489317   23.____
     WQGKAEM   2489375
     MEGKAWQ   5689324

24. XMQVSKG   6541098   24.____
     QMEKEWS   4579720
     KMEVGKG   9571983

25. GKVAMEW   88912572   25._____
    AXMVKAE   3651937
    KWAGMAV   9238531

Questions 26-35.

DIRECTIONS: Each of Questions 26 through 35 consists of a column of figures. For each question, add the column of figures and choose the correct answer from the four choices given.

26. 5,665.43   26._____
    2,356.69
    6,447.24
    7,239.65

    A. 20,698.01   B. 21,709.01
    C. 21,718.01   D. 22,609.01

27. 817,209.55   27._____
    264,354.29
     82,368.76
    849,964.89

    A. 1,893.977.49   B. 1,989,988.39
    C. 2,009,077.39   D. 2,013,897.49

28. 156,366.89   28._____
    249,973.23
    823,229.49
     56,869.45

    A. 1,286,439.06   B. 1,287,521.06
    C. 1,297,539.06   D. 1,296,421.06

29. 23,422.15   29._____
    149,696.24
    238,377.53
     86,289.79
    505,533.63

    A. 989,229.34   B. 999,879.34
    C. 1,003,330.34   D. 1,023,329.34

6 (#1)

30. 2,468,926.70
     656,842.28
     49,723.15
     832,369.59

     A. 3,218,062.72   B. 3,808,092.72
     C. 4,007,861.72   D. 4,818,192.72

30.____

31.   524,201.52
      7,775,678.51
      8,345,299.63
     40,628,898.08
     31,374,670.07

     A. 88,646,647.81   B. 88,646,747.91
     C. 88,648,647.91   D. 88,648,747.81

31.____

32. 6,824,829.40
     682,482.94
     5,542,015.27
     775,678.51
     7,732,507.25

     A. 21,557,513.37   B. 21,567,513.37
     C. 22,567,503.37   D. 22,567,513.37

32.____

33. 22,109,405.58
     6,097,093.43
     5,050,073.99
     8,118,050.05
     4,313,980.82

     A. 45,688,593.87   B. 45,688,603.87
     C. 45,689,593.87   D. 45,689,603.87

33.____

34. 79,324,114.19
     99,848,129.74
     43,331,653.31
     41,610,207.14

     A. 264,114,104.38   B. 264,114,114.38
     C. 265,114,114.38   D. 265,214,104.38

34.____

35. 33,729,653.94
    5,959,342.58
  26,052,715.47
    4,452,669.52
    7,079,953.59

A. 76,374,334.10   B. 76,375,334.10
C. 77,274,335.10   D. 77,275,335.10

35.____

Questions 36-40.

DIRECTIONS: Each of Questions 36 through 40 consists of a single number in Column I and four options in Column II. For each question, you are to choose the option (A, B, C, or D) in Column II which EXACTLY matches the number in Column I.

SAMPLE QUESTION

Column I   Column II
5965121   A. 5956121
                  B. 5965121
                  C. 5966121
                  D. 5965211

The correct answer is B. Only Option B shows the number EXACTLY as it appears in Column I. Now answer Questions 36 through 40 in the same manner.

	Column I	Column II	
36.	9643242	A. 9643242 B. 9462342 C. 9642442 D. 9463242	36.____
37.	3572477	A. 3752477 B. 3725477 C. 3572477 D. 3574277	37.____
38.	5276101	A. 5267101 B. 5726011 C. 5271601 D. 5276101	38.____
39.	4469329	A. 4496329 B. 4469329 C. 4496239 D. 4469239	39.____

40. 2326308   A. 2236308   40.____
                     B. 2233608
                     C. 2326308
                     D. 2323608

KEY (CORRECT ANSWERS)

1.	D	11.	B	21.	A	31.	D
2.	A	12.	D	22.	C	32.	A
3.	B	13.	A	23.	B	33.	B
4.	D	14.	A	24.	D	34.	A
5.	B	15.	D	25.	A	35.	C
6.	C	16.	D	26.	B	36.	A
7.	A	17.	C	27.	D	37.	C
8.	C	18.	A	28.	A	38.	D
9.	A	19.	D	29.	C	39.	B
10.	B	20.	B	30.	C	40.	C

TEST 2

DIRECTIONS: Each question or incomplete statement is followed by several suggested answers or completions. Select the one that BEST answers the question or completes the statement. *PRINT THE LETTER OF THE CORRECT ANSWER IN THE SPACE AT THE RIGHT.*

Questions 1-5.

DIRECTIONS: Each of Questions 1 through 5 consists of a name and a dollar amount. In each question, the name and dollar amount in Column II should be an EXACT copy of the name and dollar amount in Column I. If there is:
    a mistake only in the name, mark your answer A;
    a mistake only in the dollar amount, mark your answer B;
    a mistake in both the name and the dollar amount, mark your answer C;
    no mistake in either the name or the dollar amount, mark your answer D.

SAMPLE QUESTION

Column I	Column II
George Peterson	George Petersson
$125.50	$125.50

Compare the name and dollar amount in Column II with the name and dollar amount in Column I. The name *Petersson* in Column II is spelled *Peterson* in Column I. The amount is the same in both columns. Since there is a mistake only in the name, the answer to the sample question is A. Now answer Questions 1 through 5 in the same manner.

	Column I	Column II	
1.	Susanne Shultz $3440	Susanne Schultz $3440	1.____
2.	Anibal P. Contrucci $2121.61	Anibel P. Contrucci $2112.61	2.____
3.	Eugenio Mendoza $12.45	Eugenio Mendozza $12.45	3.____
4.	Maurice Gluckstadt $4297	Maurice Gluckstadt $4297	4.____
5.	John Pampellonne $4656.94	John Pammpellonne $4566.94	5.____

Questions 6-11.

DIRECTIONS: Each of Questions 6 through 11 consist of a set of names and addresses, which you are to compare. In each question, the name and addresses in Column II should be an EXACT copy of the name and address in Column I. If there is:
- a mistake only in the name, mark your answer A;
- a mistake only in the address, mark your answer B;
- a mistake in both the name and address, mark your answer C;
- no mistake in either the name or address, mark your answer D.

SAMPLE QUESTION

Column I
Michael Filbert
456 Reade Street
New York, N.Y. 10013

Column II
Michael Filbert
645 Reade Street
New York, N.Y. 10013

Since there is a mistake only in the address (the street number should be 456 instead of 645), the answer to the sample question is B. Now answer Questions 6 through 11 in the same manner.

	Column I	Column II	
6.	Hilda Goettelmann 55 Lenox Rd. Brooklyn, N.Y. 11226	Hilda Goetteleman 55 Lenox Ave. Brooklyn, N.Y. 11226	6.____
7.	Arthur Sherman 2522 Batchelder St. Brooklyn, N.Y. 11235	Arthur Sharman 2522 Batcheder St. Brooklyn, N.Y. 11253	7.____
8.	Ralph Barnett 300 West 28 Street New York, New York 10001	Ralph Barnett 300 West 28 Street New York, New York 10001	8.____
9.	George Goodwin 135 Palmer Avenue Staten Island, New York 10302	George Godwin 135 Palmer Avenue Staten Island, New York 10302	9.____
10.	Alonso Ramirez 232 West 79 Street New York, N.Y. 10024	Alonso Ramirez 223 West 79 Street New York, N.Y. 10024	10.____
11.	Cynthia Graham 149-34 83 Street Howard Beach, N.Y. 11414	Cynthia Graham 149-35 83 Street Howard Beach, N.Y. 11414	11.____

3 (#2)

Questions 12-20.

DIRECTIONS: Questions 12 through 20 are problems in subtraction. For each question do the subtraction and select your answer from the four choices given.

12. 232,921.85
     -179,587.68

   A. 52,433.17   B. 52,434.17
   C. 53,334.17   D. 53,343,17

12._____

13. 5,531,876.29
     -3,897,158.36

   A. 1,634,717.93   B. 1,644,718.93
   C. 1,734,717.93   D. 1,7234,718.93

13._____

14. 1,482,658.22
     -937,925.76

   A. 544,633.46   B. 544,732.46
   C. 545,632.46   D. 545,732.46

14._____

15. 937,828.17
     -259,673.88

   A. 678,154.29   B. 679,154.29
   C. 688,155.39   D. 699,155.39

15._____

16. 760,412.38
     -263,465.95

   A. 496,046.43   B. 496,946.43
   C. 496,956.43   D. 497,046.43

16._____

17. 3,203,902.26
     -2,933,087.96

   A. 260,814.30   B. 269,824.30
   C. 270,814.30   D. 270,824.30

17._____

18. 1,023,468.71
     -934,678.88

   A. 88,780.83   B. 88,789.83
   C. 88,880.83   D. 88,889.83

18._____

19. 831,549.47
    -772,814.78

    A. 58,734.69 B. 58,834.69
    C. 59,735.69 D. 59,834.69

20. 6,306,181.74
    -3,617,376.99

    A. 2,687,904.99 B. 2,688,904.99
    C. 2,689,804.99 D. 2,799,905.99

Questions 21-30.

DIRECTIONS: Each of Questions 21 through 30 consists of three lines of code letters and three lines of numbers. The numbers on each line should correspond with the code letters on the same line in accordance with the table below.

Code Letter	J	U	B	T	Y	D	K	R	L	P
Corresponding Number	0	1	2	3	4	5	6	7	8	9

On some of the lines, an error exists in the coding. Compare the letters and numbers in each question carefully. If you find an error or errors on:
only *one* of the lines in the question, mark your answer A;
any *two* lines in the question, mark your answer B;
all *three* lines in the question, mark your answer C;
none of the lines in the question, mark your answer D.

SAMPLE QUESTION

BJRPYUR   2079417
DTBPYKJ   5328460
YKLDBLT   4685283

In the above sample, the first line is correct since each code letter listed has the correct corresponding number. On the second line, an error exists because code letter P should have the number 9 instead of the number 8. The third line is correct since each code letter listed has the correct corresponding number. Since there is an error in *one* of the three lines, the correct answer is A. Now answer Questions 21 through 30 in the same manner.

21. BYPDTJL   2495308
    PLRDTJU   9815301
    DTJRYLK   5207486

22. RPBYRJK   7934706
    PKTYLBU   9624821
    KDLPJYR   6489047

23.	TPYBUJR	3942107	23.____
	BYRKPTU	2476931	
	DUKPYDL	5169458	
24.	KBYDLPL	6345898	24.____
	BLRKBRU	2876261	
	JTULDYB	0318542	
25.	LDPYDKR	8594567	25.____
	BDKDRJL	2565708	
	BDRPLUJ	2679810	
26.	PLRLBPU	9858291	26.____
	LPYKRDJ	88936750	
	TDKPDTR	3569527	
27.	RKURPBY	7617924	27.____
	RYUKPTJ	7426930	
	RTKPTJD	7369305	
28.	DYKPBJT	5469203	28.____
	KLPJBTL	6890238	
	TKPLBJP	3698209	
29.	BTPRJYL	2397148	29.____
	LDKUTYR	8561347	
	YDBLRPJ	4528190	
30.	ULPBKYT	1892643	30.____
	KPDTRBJ	6953720	
	YLKJPTB	4860932	

KEY (CORRECT ANSWERS)

1.	A	11.	D	21.	B
2.	C	12.	C	22.	C
3.	A	13.	A	23.	D
4.	D	14.	B	24.	B
5.	C	15.	A	25.	A
6.	C	16.	B	26.	C
7.	C	17.	C	27.	A
8.	D	18.	B	28.	D
9.	A	19.	A	29.	B
10.	B	20.	B	30.	D

NAME AND NUMBER CHECKING
EXAMINATION SECTION
TEST 1

DIRECTIONS: This test is designed to measure your speed/and accuracy. You are urged to work both quickly and accurately and to do correctly as many lists as you can in the time allowed. The test consists of lists or pairs of names and numbers. Count the number of IDENTICAL pairs in each list. Then, select the correct number, 1, 2, 3, 4, 5, and indicate your choice in the space at the right. Two sample questions are presented for your guidance, together with the correct solutions.

SAMPLE LIST A
Adelphi College – Adelphia College
Braxton Corp – Braxeton Corp.
Wassaic State School – Wassaic State School
Central Islip State Hospital – Central Isllip State Hospital
Greenwich House – Greenwich House

NOTE: There are only two correct pairs—Wassaic State School and Greenwich House. Therefore, the CORRECT answer is 2.

SAMPLE LIST B
78453694 – 78453684
784530 – 784530
533 – 534
67845 – 67845
2368745 – 2368755

NOTE: There are only two correct pairs—784530 and 67845. Therefore, the CORRECT answer is 2.

LIST 1   1.____
    Diagnostic Clinic   – Diagnostic Clinic
    Yorkville Health   – Yorkville Health
    Meinhard Clinic   – Meinhart Clinic
    Corlears Clinic   – Carlears Clinic
    Tremont Diagnostic   – Tremont Diagnostic

LIST 2   2.____
    73526   – 73526
    7283627198   – 7283627198
    627   – 637
    728352617283   – 7283526178282
    6281   – 6281

2 (#1)

LIST 3　　　　　　　　　　　　　　　　　　　　　　　　　　　　　　　　　3._____
    Jefferson Clinic   – Jeffersen Clinic
    Mott Haven Center   – Mott Havan Center
    Bronx Hospital   – Bronx Hospital
    Montefiore Hospital   – Montifeore Hospital
    Beth Isreal Hospital – Beth Israel Hospital

LIST 4　　　　　　　　　　　　　　　　　　　　　　　　　　　　　　　　　4._____
    936271826   – 936371826
    5271   – 5291
    82637192037   – 82637192037
    527182   – 5271882
    726354256   - 72635456

LIST 5　　　　　　　　　　　　　　　　　　　　　　　　　　　　　　　　　5._____
    Trinity Hospital   – Trinity Hospital
    Central Harlem   – Centrel Harlem
    St. Luke's Hospital   – St. Lukes' Hospital
    Mt. Sinai Hospital   – Mt. Sinia Hospital
    N.Y. Dispensery   – N.Y. Dispensary

LIST 6　　　　　　　　　　　　　　　　　　　　　　　　　　　　　　　　　6._____
    725361552637   – 725361555637
    7526378   – 7526377
    6975   – 6975
    82637481028   – 82637481028
    3427   – 3429

LIST 7　　　　　　　　　　　　　　　　　　　　　　　　　　　　　　　　　7._____
    Misericordia Hospital – Miseracordia Hospital
    Lebonan Hospital   – Lebanon Hospital
    Gouverneur Hospital – Gouverner Hospital
    German Polyclinic   – German Policlinic
    French Hospital   – French Hospital

LIST 8　　　　　　　　　　　　　　　　　　　　　　　　　　　　　　　　　8._____
    8277364933251   – 827364933351
    63728   – 63728
    367281   – 367281
    62733846273   – 6273846293
    62836   - 6283

LIST 9　　　　　　　　　　　　　　　　　　　　　　　　　　　　　　　　　9._____
    King's County Hospital – Kings County Hospital
    St. Johns Long Island – St. John's Long Island
    Bellevue Hospital   – Bellvue Hospital
    Beth David Hospital – Beth David Hospital
    Samaritan Hospital   – Samariton Hospital

3 (#1)

LIST 10   10.____
    62836454   – 62836455
    42738267   – 42738369
    573829   – 573829
    738291627874   – 738291627874
    725   - 735

LIST 11   11.____
    Bloomingdal Clinic   – Bloomingdale Clinic
    Communitty Hospital   – Community Hospital
    Metroplitan Hospital   – Metropoliton Hospital
    Lenox Hill Hospital   – Lonex Hill Hospital
    Lincoln Hospital   – Lincoln Hospital

LIST 12   12.____
    6283364728   – 6283648
    627385   – 627383
    54283902   – 54283602
    63354   – 63354
    7283562781   - 7283562781

LIST 13   13.____
    Sydenham Hospital   – Sydanham Hospital
    Roosevalt Hospital   – Roosevelt Hospital
    Vanderbilt Clinic   – Vanderbild Clinic
    Women's Hospital   – Woman's Hospital
    Flushing Hospital   – Flushing Hospital

LIST 14   14.____
    62738   – 62738
    727355542321   – 72735542321
    263849332   – 263849332
    262837   – 263837
    47382912   - 47382922

LIST 15   15.____
    Episcopal Hospital   – Episcapal Hospital
    Flower Hospital   – Flouer Hospital
    Stuyvesent Clinic   – Stuyvesant Clinic
    Jamaica Clinic   – Jamaica Clinic
    Ridgwood Clinic   – Ridgewood Clinic

LIST 16   16.____
    628367299   – 628367399
    111   – 111
    118293304829   – 1182839489
    4448   – 4448
    333693678   - 333693678

4 (#1)

LIST 17
    Arietta Crane Farm   – Areitta Crane Farm
    Bikur Chilim Home   – Bikur Chilom Home
    Burke Foundation   – Burke Foundation
    Blythedale Home   – Blythdale Home
    Campbell Cottages   – Cambell Cottages

17.____

LIST 18
    32123   – 32132
    273893326783   – 27389326783
    473829   – 473829
    7382937   – 7383937
    3628890122332   - 36289012332

18.____

LIST 19
    Caraline Rest   – Caroline Rest
    Loreto Rest   – Loretto Rest
    Edgewater Creche   – Edgwater Creche
    Holiday Farm   – Holiday Farm
    House of St. Giles   – House of st. Giles

19.____

LIST 20
    557286777   – 55728677
    3678902   – 3678892
    1567839   – 1567839
    7865434712   – 7865344712
    9927382   - 9927382

20.____

LIST 21
    Isabella Home   – Isabela Home
    James A. Moore Home   – James A. More Home
    The Robin's Nest   – The Roben's Nest
    Pelham Home   – Pelam Home
    St. Eleanora's Home   – St. Eleanora's Home

21.____

LIST 22
    273648293048   – 273648293048
    334   – 334
    7362536478   – 7362536478
    7362819273   – 7362819273
    7362   - 7363

22.____

LIST 23
    St. Pheobe's Mission   – St. Phebe's Mission
    Seaside Home   – Seaside Home
    Speedwell Society   – Speedwell Society
    Valeria Home   – Valera Home
    Wiltwyck   - Wildwyck

23.____

5 (#1)

LIST 24   24.____
   63728   – 63738
   63728192736   – 63728192738
   428   – 458
   62738291527   – 62738291529
   63728192   - 63728192

LIST 25   25.____
   McGaffin   – McGafin
   David Ardslee   – David Ardslee
   Axton Supply   – Axeton Supply Co
   Alice Russell   – Alice Russell
   Dobson Mfg. Co.   – Dobsen Mfg. Co.

KEY (CORRECT ANSWERS)

1.	3		11.	1
2.	3		12.	2
3.	1		13.	1
4.	1		14.	2
5.	1		15.	1
6.	2		16.	3
7.	1		17.	1
8.	2		18.	1
9.	1		19.	1
10.	2		20.	2

21.	1
22.	4
23.	2
24.	1
25.	2

TEST 2

DIRECTIONS: This test is designed to measure your speed/and accuracy. You are urged to work both quickly and accurately and to do correctly as many lists as you can in the time allowed. The test consists of lists or pairs of names and numbers. Count the number of IDENTICAL pairs in each list. Then, select the correct number, 1, 2, 3, 4, 5, and indicate your choice in the space at the right.

LIST 1   1.____
    82637381028   – 82637281028
    928   – 928
    72937281028   – 72937281028
    7362   – 7362
    927382615   – 927382615

LIST 2   2.____
    Albee Theatre   – Albee Theatre
    Lapland Lumber Co.   – Laplund Lumber Co.
    Adelphi College   – Adelphi College
    Jones & Son Inc.   – Jones & Sons Inc.
    S.W. Ponds Co.   – S.W. Ponds Co.

LIST 3   3.____
    85345   – 85345
    895643278   – 895643277
    726352   – 726353
    632685   – 632685
    7263524   – 7236524

LIST 4   4.____
    Eagle Library   – Eagle Library
    Dodge Ltd.   – Dodge Co.
    Stromberg Carlson   – Stromberg Carlsen
    Clairice Ling   – Clairice Linng
    Mason Book Co.   – Matson Book Co.

LIST 5   5.____
    66273   – 66273
    629   – 629
    7382517283   – 7382517283
    637281   – 639281
    2738261   – 2788261

LIST 6   6.____
    Robert MacColl   – Robert McColl
    Buick Motor   – Buck Motors
    Murray Bay & Co. Ltd. – Murray Bay Co. Ltd.
    L.T. Ltyle   – L.T. Lyttle
    A.S. Landas   – A.S. Landas

2 (#2)

LIST 7   7._____
    6271526374890   – 627152637490
    73526189   – 73526189
    5372   – 5392
    637281142   – 63728124
    4783946   – 4783046

LIST 8   8._____
    Tyndall Burke   – Tyndell Burke
    W. Briehl   – W. Briehl
    Burritt Publishing Co. – Buritt Publishing Co.
    Frederick Breyer & Co. – Frederick Breyer Co.
    Bailey Buulard   – Bailey Bullard

LIST 9   9._____
    634   – 634
    16837   – 163837
    273892223678   – 27389223678
    527182   – 527782
    3628901223   – 3629002223

LIST 10   10._____
    Ernest Boas   – Ernest Boas
    Rankin Barne   – Rankin Barnes
    Edward Appley   – Edward Appely
    Camel   – Camel
    Caiger Food Co.   – Caiger Food Co.

LIST 11   11._____
    6273   – 6273
    322   – 332
    15672839   – 15672839
    63728192637   – 63728192639
    738   – 738

LIST 12   12._____
    Wells Fargo Co.   – Wells Fargo Co.
    W.D. Brett   – W.D. Britt
    Tassco Co.   – Tassko Co.
    Republic Mills   – Republic Mill
    R.W. Burnham   – R.W. Burhnam

LIST 13   13._____
    7253529152   – 7283529152
    6283   – 6383
    52839102738   – 5283910238
    308   – 398
    82637201927   – 8263720127

LIST 14
Schumacker Co.   – Shumacker Co.
C.H. Caiger   – C.H. Caiger
Abraham Strauss   – Abram Straus
B.F. Boettjer   – B.F. Boettijer
Cut-Rate Store   – Cut-Rate Stores

14.____

LIST 15
15273826   – 15273826
72537   – 73537
726391027384   – 62639107384
637389   – 627399
725382910   – 725382910

15.____

LIST 16
Hixby Ltd.   – Hixby Lt'd.
S. Reiner   – S. Riener
Reynard Co.   – Reynord Co.
Esso Gassoline Co.   – Esso Gasolene Co.
Belle Brock   – Belle Brock

16.____

LIST 17
7245   – 7245
819263728192   – 819263728172
682537289   – 682537298
789   – 789
82936542891   – 82936542891

17.____

LIST 18
Joseph Cartwright   – Joseph Cartwrite
Foote Food Co.   – Foot Food Co.
Weiman & Held   – Weiman & Held
Sanderson Shoe Co.   – Sandersen Shoe Co.
A.M. Byrne   – A.N. Byrne

18.____

LIST 19
4738267   – 4738277
63728   – 63729
6283628901   – 6283628991
918264   – 918264
263728192037   – 2637728192073

19.____

LIST 20
Exray Laboratories   – Exray Labratories
Curley Toy Co.   – Curly Toy Co.
J. Lauer & Cross   – J. Laeur & Cross
Mireco Brands   – Mireco Brands
Sandor Lorand   – Sandor Larand

20.____

4 (#2)

LIST 21   21.____
    607   – 609
    6405   – 6403
    976   – 996
    101267   – 101267
    2065432   – 20965432

LIST 22   22.____
    John Macy & Sons   – John Macy & Son
    Venus Pencil Co.   – Venus Pencil Co.
    Nell McGinnis   – Nell McGinnis
    McCutcheon & Co.   – McCutcheon & Co.
    Sun-Tan Oil   – Sun-Tan Oil

LIST 23   23.____
    703345700   – 703345700
    46754   – 466754
    3367490   – 3367490
    3379   – 3778
    47384   – 47394

LIST 24   24.____
    arthritis   – arthritis
    asthma   – asthma
    endocrine   – endocrene
    gastro-enterological – gastrol-enteralogical
    orthopedic   – orthopedic

LIST 25   25.____
    743829432   – 743828432
    998   – 998
    732816253902   – 732816252902
    46829   – 46830
    7439120249   – 7439210249

KEY (CORRECT ANSWERS)

1.	4	11.	3
2.	3	12.	1
3.	2	13.	1
4.	1	14.	1
5.	2	15.	2
6.	1	16.	1
7.	2	17.	3
8.	1	18.	1
9.	1	19.	1
10.	3	20.	1

21.	1
22.	4
23.	2
24.	3
25.	1

www.ingramcontent.com/pod-product-compliance
Lightning Source LLC
Chambersburg PA
CBHW080322020526
44117CB00035B/2597